FROM COTTON FIELDS TO COURTROOMS

A Texas Lawyer's Memoir

THOMAS R. CONNER

From Cotton Fields to Courtrooms
A Texas Lawyer's Memoir
by Thomas R. Conner
Copyright © 2025 Thomas R. Conner
Published by SkillBites LLC
www.skillbites.net
All rights reserved.

No part of this book may be reproduced or transmitted in any form or by any means whatsoever without written permission from the author, except in the case of brief quotations embodied in critical articles and reviews.

DISCLAIMER

While the publisher and author have used their best efforts in preparing this book, they make no representations or warranties with respect to the accuracy or completeness of the contents of this book. Neither the publisher nor the author shall be liable for any loss of profit or any other commercial damages, including but not limited to special, incidental, consequential, or other damages.

Internet addresses given in this book were accurate at the time it went to press.

Printed in the United States of America

For more information or to place bulk orders, contact the author or the publisher at info@skillbites.net.

Photo of Emerald Lake by Jack Brauer.

ISBN: 978-1-952281-89-1 eBook
ISBN: 978-1-952281-88-4 paperback

To Anne, Emily, and Will

Table of Contents

Introduction. 1

1 The Baron and the Cohn Job 3

2 The Beginning 15

3 Moving On. 21

4 My First Job 25

5 Return to West Texas 29

6 The Radio Years 33

7 The Big Stick. 39

8 The University. 45

9 Six Coeds in a VW Bus. 53

10 Europe Lessons Learned 61

11 Number 365 69

12 Highs and Lows in Law School. 73

13 Anne. 77

14 The Bookie Murder. 81

15 The Blue Law Cases 93

16 The Bed Rolled Out 113

17 The Disbarred Judge 117

18 The Worst Day of My Law Practice. 125

19 The Richest Man Ever Tried for Murder 129

20 You Can't Win 'Em All 143

21 The Shyster Lawyer 147

22 Kidnapping in the Middle East. 151

23 The Most Famous Name in Football. 159

24 More Tales 167

25 Emily 195

26 The TIRR Emily Endowment. 203

EPILOGUE It's Been Quite a Ride 209

Acknowledgments 211

Introduction

I'M A LAWYER. OVER THE YEARS, I'VE told "war stories" from my forty-five years of practice. The headnotes and footnotes to these legal dramatic and light-hearted memories often included tales from my younger days. When sharing some of these stories, I often heard those encouraging words: "You need to write a book."

I found in writing these stories, personal and professional, they were inevitably intertwined. So, in essence, you readers are getting two books in one.

So here we go!

1

The Baron and the Cohn Job

HUGH ROY CULLEN WAS A TEXAS OILMAN known as the King of the Wildcatters. Born in 1881, he grew up in poverty in San Antonio. He dropped out of the fifth grade to go to work supporting his mother. At age eighteen, he became a cotton buyer in Texas and Oklahoma. Coming to Houston in 1911, he enjoyed continued success and earned a seat on the Houston Cotton Exchange.

By 1917, the relatively new field of oil exploration caught his eye, specifically creekology—detecting oil by studying surface geology and the paths of flowing water around land formations. He partnered with another wildcatter, Jim Creek. Though both had little experience in oil exploration, they struck oil at Pierce Junction, now part of the City of Houston. Where others had failed, Cullen drilled through the shale and produced 5,000 barrels of oil a day. Cullen and Creek sold their interests to Humble Oil, now Exxon. With his share of the money, Cullen went out on his own.

Cullen's legend took root in 1934 when he discovered the Tom O'Connor oil field near Victoria, ninety miles southwest of Houston, so rich with oil that it is still producing today as I write this in 2024. It made Mr. Cullen an extremely wealthy man, amassing his holdings under the name Quintana Petroleum.

In 1938, Cullen divided the interests and oil fields of Quintana Petroleum among trusts for his four daughters and their children. Cullen's new company, Quintana Products, was then drilling for oil and carrying out exploration on the fields owned by the trusts. In 1954, three years before his death, his fortune was estimated at $2.5 billion in today's dollars.

Lillie Cullen was his oldest daughter. As a young woman, she moved to Los Angeles, perhaps to escape the small-town environment of Houston. Although it is the fourth-largest city in the country today, Houston was small in the '20s with a population of 200,000. In hindsight, considering subsequent events in her life, it seems she likely suffered from mental health issues. And in Los Angeles, Lillie met a handsome, struggling Italian actor named Paolo di Portanova.

Paolo held himself out as Baron di Portanova, but he was not a baron, nor was di Portanova his real name. It was Apuzzo. His first wife was a di Portanova. After divorcing her, he decided that her name was more regal than Apuzzo, so he adopted it.

Lillie and Paolo married, and in 1934, they had their first son, Enrico, or "Ricky." Two years later, Lillie gave birth to a second son, Ugo. Mr. Cullen brought the di Portanova family to Houston and gave Paolo a job with Quintana, which proved a terrible idea. Paolo had no work ethic, business knowledge, or desire to improve in either category. The di Portanovas returned to California, divorcing soon after. Paolo got primary guardianship of the boys at a time when fathers seldom, if ever, got custody of their children.

When Ugo was twelve, he spent the summer with his mother. When he returned to Paolo, he was diagnosed with schizophrenia and suffered from it for the rest of his life. After that, Ricky and Ugo lost contact with their mother, and Ugo lived permanently in Italy with Paolo.

As an adult, Ricky lived in Rome, working in the jewelry business. In the early 1960s, he moved to Houston to claim his Cullen heritage and introduced himself as the new incarnation of Baron di Portanova. He initially received $5,000 a month from the Cullen estate, but by the early 1980s, that sum had increased to $1.2 million a month.

In 1967, Ricky started proceedings to have Ugo declared legally incapacitated, succeeding in being named the guardian of Ugo's share of the Cullen fortune. Ricky now controlled Ugo's money on a scale equal to Ricky's, as both were beneficiaries of various Cullen trusts.

Ricky was a jet-setter with homes in Houston, Italy, and Mexico. He referred to his Lear jet as his "taxi." He and his wife Sandra, the daughter of a furniture store owner in Houston, carried so much luggage that many times their servants had to fly commercially.

The di Portanova residence in Acapulco was a spectacular villa named Arabesque. At that time, it was reputed to be the largest home in Mexico. The house had twenty-eight bedrooms, twenty-six baths, and five kitchens. Ricky needed the kitchens, having been proud of his culinary skills, specializing in pasta tossed with caviar. Arabesque also included four swimming pools, indoor waterfalls, a nightclub, a tower manned by guards, and a rooftop helicopter landing pad. The house was used as a backdrop in the James Bond movie *License to Kill*.

On a flight returning from Mexico in the '80s, my seatmate was a doctor from Acapulco. We started talking about Ricky. Although this story may be apocryphal, the doctor said that when

Ricky was building Arabesque, he met with the architects and told them to triple the size. He thought the measurements were in feet. They were in meters.

In the early '80s, Ricky was a frequent visitor to New York, where he met the infamous lawyer Roy Cohn, when Ricky was trying to buy the 21 Club for Sandra's birthday.

Cohn was counsel to Senator Joe McCarthy's infamous Army-McCarthy Senate committee and was instrumental in instigating the Red Scare of the early '50s. Cohn was variously described as a "snake," a "scoundrel," and a "new strain of a son of a bitch." He was as notorious for his immoral behavior as he was for his clients, including the owners of Studio 54 and a New York real estate developer named Donald Trump. He taught Trump to "Attack, attack, attack. Deny everything, admit nothing, always hit back, never apologize, and always claim victory." Trump apparently learned those lessons well. A frustrated President Trump would later lament, "Where's my Roy Cohn?"

In 1986, Cohn was disbarred for convincing an incapacitated client to amend his will. The new will bequeathed a sizeable estate to Cohn.

By 1978, Quintana was run by Cullen's son-in-law, Corbin Robertson, Sr. The family still held all its investments in respective trusts, which were heavily invested in Quintana. Consequently, the family fortune continued to grow. The Cullen family members would make joint decisions about investments and opportunities that were presented to them. Ricky and Ugo were not included.

Ricky complained to Cohn about this slight. Cohn, ever-present with good or bad legal guidance, advised Ricky to sue the Cullens based on a legal theory he captioned "family opportunity." He told Ricky that when an opportunity presented itself to Quintana, the family had a duty to advise him and invite his participation.

Ricky, anxious to be treated as an equal Cullen heir, hired Cohn to file suit against his Cullen relatives. Ugo, Ricky's incapacitated brother, became a necessary party because his interests were the same as Ricky's. If Cohn and Ricky were right, Ugo was also entitled to his additional share of the Cullen fortune. Because he was mentally incapacitated, the suit was brought in Harris County Probate Court, the court that had declared Ugo incompetent.

With that filing, my partner, James Patrick Smith, and I were thrust into a legal maelstrom, as J.P. was appointed by the probate judge to be Ugo's lawyer. Due to the complexity of this litigation, it was necessary that I become intimately involved in the case.

The other parties to the litigation were the Cullen family, the trusts, and several of the major banks in Houston acting as trustees. Vinson and Elkins, a prominent Houston firm, represented the Cullen family. The family members also hired Joe Jamail, the King of Torts. Joe had famously prevailed in the record $11 billion verdict in *Pennzoil v. Texaco*, which forced Texaco into bankruptcy.

J.P. and I were acutely aware that this was a complex case and that his role—and mine as his law partner—would require legal work and footwork.

One of our initial jobs was to examine Ricky's role as Ugo's trustee over one of the trusts. It was soon determined he had used Ugo's money for his personal expenses. One example: Ricky used Ugo's checkbook to buy a jet helicopter, flying up and down the Italian coast. In less than a year, Ricky was removed as trustee of that trust. A bank was put in his place. As a result, more than $2.5 million was recovered from Ricky.

Cohn knew that the trial judge had confidence in us since he appointed J.P. as Ugo's lawyer. Cohn invited us to New York to strategize. As Ugo's lawyers, it was incumbent on us to join forces with Cohn. If his legal theory was correct, Ugo would gain a substantial amount of money.

Flying to New York, Cohn's limousine picked us up at La Guardia and took us to his office/apartment on the Upper East Side. We worked hard during the day. At night, Cohn made sure that we were given a royal New York experience. We enjoyed dinner on the second floor of the 21 Club—traditionally reserved for wealthy and famous customers—orchestra seats for the Broadway show *Sugar Babies,* starring Mickey Rooney, and an evening at Studio 54, the hottest club in New York at that time.

On Saturday, with Cohn's associate as our guide, we visited Little Italy for the Feast of San Genaro. This celebration was prominently featured in *The Godfather Part II* when a young Vito Corleone assassinates the white-suited godfather of Little Italy. Of course, we enjoyed Cohn's hospitality.

Ugo was a fascinating person, fluent in Italian and English. He was a patron of the arts who enjoyed opera as well as *Mister Rogers' Neighborhood.* At ease with one or two people, he would become very agitated in a group. Being alone with him one day, we had a lively discussion about current events. He was well-informed, articulate, and intelligent. I also found him to be a very nice man who hated the litigation and thought talking about money was silly.

Another player in this drama was Ugo's father, Paolo. After Ugo was declared incompetent, Paolo became the guardian of his person, meaning Paolo looked after Ugo's daily personal needs. Paolo employed a young couple, Jake and Tina LaMatta, to assist him. Ugo was highly attached to Tina, who was very kind to him.

Paolo was an unintended beneficiary of the Cullen fortune as Ugo's trusts would provide him money as requested for Ugo's needs. Because of Ugo's wealth, these needs included not only maintaining his lifestyle in Italy but also a luxury apartment in Monte Carlo, a penthouse in a high-rise on Memorial Drive in Houston, and a farm in Austin County, Texas. The LaMattas lived with Ugo in Texas, while Paolo spent most of his time in Italy.

The court and the trustees were in a quandary. Paolo was constantly requesting large sums of funds for Ugo, and the trustees were aware that Paolo and his wife were living a lavish lifestyle on Ugo's tab. When asked for an accounting, Paolo usually provided insufficient information. His constant response begged incredulity: "It's difficult to get proper paperwork and receipts in Italy." Ugo was worth $50 million in the mid-80s, and he had the right to enjoy his money. Paolo had no hesitation enjoying it too.

It came to light that Paolo had purchased a yacht for Ugo that was berthed in the harbor at Monte Carlo. The court became suspicious that this multimillion-dollar purchase was a sham. The court ordered J.P. and me to fly to Monte Carlo to find the yacht. And we did.

We arrived at the Nice, France, airport and were driven to the Monte Carlo apartment where Paolo, his wife, and Ugo lived. It was magnificent, with fine art and antique furniture. The view from the living room was of the beautiful gardens facing the famous casino's facade. It was a breathtaking sight. We had a sumptuous dinner with Ugo, Paolo, and his wife, joined by the LaMattas. Paolo announced that we would board the yacht the next morning and go to Portofino, Italy. The yacht was in the Monte Carlo yacht basin, directly behind the Hotel de Paris. The captain and four crew members greeted us. In the main cabin was an original Monet, with ample room for a dozen people. The four staterooms all had full baths with bidets. It was magnificent. We examined the paperwork and found it in order as to the ownership for the benefit of Ugo.

We had a lovely day trip across the Mediterranean to the quaint Italian resort city of Portofino. I went to the yacht's bridge and visited with the captain. Upon noticing that no one was at the ship's wheel, the captain informed me that a computer controlled the yacht. We were on autopilot. It was cutting-edge technology for 1983.

We arrived in Portofino and had dinner with our group, facing the beautiful harbor. The next morning, J.P. and I boarded the train for Rome. We stayed at a hotel on the trendy Via Veneto. Italy had won the World Cup that night. Sitting outside enjoying our drinks, the street was overcome with gloriously happy Italians celebrating their victory.

As to the lawsuit, the show belonged to Roy Cohn and Joe Jamail. Because of Cohn's involvement, the case was national news. It did not take Joe much time or encouragement to overshadow him. At one of Cohn's news conferences, which he liked to hold, Joe—having learned that Cohn had not tried a case in fifteen years—showed up to gleefully interrupt Cohn in front of the media. Looking into Cohn's face, in full view of the television cameras, Joe said, "I found out you haven't tried a case in over a decade. I'm going to need all the cowboys and barbed wire in Texas to get you into that courtroom."

When we took Paolo's deposition, Cohn asked Joe not to mention that Paolo was not a baron. Knowing that humiliating Paolo would add nothing to the case, Joe complied. Ricky's deposition was a different story.

When Ricky was deposed, Joe called him Enrico. Ricky said, "I would appreciate it if you called me Baron."

Jamail smiled and said, "I'm an American. I would be happy to refer to you as 'asshole,' if you prefer." Typical Jamail.

Cohn's "family opportunity" legal theory was borrowed from the legal theory of "loss of business opportunity." An example: If a partnership invested in real estate and one partner came upon an opportunity to buy land, that partner would have to share the opportunity with the other partners. If he failed to do so, then purchased the property on his own and was successful, the partner would owe the other partners the money that should have been their share of the profits.

Though Cohn's theory was inventive, it would have to break new ground in Texas. In many instances, that is how new case law is made—but not in this case. Vinson and Elkins filed a 226-page motion for summary judgment. In the simplest terms, a motion for summary judgment tells the court that Ricky could not recover on the facts and the law. The court granted the motion. The case was over.

To be involved with such great legal talent, larger than life personalities, amazing facts, and massive wealth in a case that was making weekly headlines was an unforgettable experience. I learned a lot and became good friends with a legendary lawyer, Jamail.

Ricky appealed the court's decision. Joe was sitting in the court, waiting to hear the oral arguments by the appellate lawyers. A New York lawyer, representing Ricky, walked in and asked who Joe Jamail was. Joe noticed the lawyer had a backpack on and nodded, "I'm Jamail. Why are you wearing a backpack?" The lawyer responded that he had just come in from the airport. Joe replied, "You better wear it a lot lower if you know what part of your anatomy I'm coming after."

While Joe's remarks are harsh on paper, he said them with a glint in his eye. His purposeful behavior was to throw people off balance. A prominent white-collar New York lawyer had never been treated like this. It could take his mind off the case.

In another case, I defended a doctor in a medical malpractice suit brought by Joe's law partner Gus Kolius. Gus, an incredibly talented lawyer in his own right, was taking the doctor's deposition. The doctor was doing fine as a witness when Jamail walked in and sat down.

"Doctor, my name is Joe Jamail. Do you mind if I ask you some questions?"

The doctor turned into a terrible witness. Jamail was the most famous lawyer in Texas. My client became severely intimidated. To add to that, Joe was a tough examiner. The doctor might have confessed to murder if Joe had asked him. Joe had that effect on people.

And what happened to all the characters in the di Portanova saga?

Hugh Roy Cullen died of natural causes in 1957, leaving much of his fortune to the Cullen Foundation, supporting worthwhile causes including the University of Houston and Baylor College of Medicine.

Lillie Cullen di Portanova struggled with mental health issues and was eventually declared incompetent. In her later years, Ricky, in legal maneuverings, had her competency restored. She then signed a will leaving her share of the Cullen fortune to her sons. She died a bag lady in New York in 1982. In her room, a mattress was found stuffed with cash.

Ricky di Portanova died in Houston of lung cancer in 2000. His wife, Sandra, had died several months earlier. Ricky's health was so precarious that he never learned of her death.

Ugo di Portanova, now in his eighties, lives with his incompetence and has not regained the power to manage his affairs. After the Cullen case, four new trustees were appointed to manage his wealth. They took financial advantage of Ugo and were ultimately removed as well.

Roy Cohn was diagnosed with AIDS and attempted to keep his condition secret. While he decried homosexuality, it was later learned that he was gay. He insisted to his dying day, at age fifty-nine in 1986, that his disease was liver cancer. Ironically, his old boss, Senator Joe McCarthy, was known for his hatred of homosexuals. At his death, the IRS seized most of Cohn's assets.

One of the things that the IRS did not seize was a pair of diamond cufflinks, a gift from his client and friend Donald Trump.

Joe Jamail died in 2015 as the wealthiest practicing attorney in the United States, worth $1.5 billion. He and his wife Lee were extremely generous in their contributions to Rice University, the University of Texas, and Baylor College of Medicine, among others. I visited with Joe a few months before his death. It was sad, as he commented that all his friends of his generation had gone before him. He continued to grieve for Lee, who predeceased him.

Paolo di Portanova was removed as guardian of Ugo's person in 1987. After additional accounting—or lack thereof—Paolo was determined to have squandered $18 million of Ugo's money. Ugo's new guardian of his person became his caregiver, Tina LaMatta. Paolo died a few years later.

But the courtrooms in Houston were a long way from my roots in the cotton fields of West Texas.

2

The Beginning

LEGEND HAS IT THAT FAMOUS COMANCHE CHIEF Quanah Parker was born a few miles from my parents' 160-acre cotton farm on the Seminole Highway, just west of Lamesa. A small brick farmhouse was my first home in this farming community in Dawson County, Texas. The year was 1948.

Sixty miles south of Lubbock, Dawson County is the southern tip of the *Llano Estacado*, the Staked Plains, covering over 37,000 square miles. The land is so flat that early explorers drove stakes in the ground to find their way back to where they started. When Coronado first explored this region for Spain in 1541, he wrote, "I reached some plains so vast, that I did not find their limit anywhere I went, although I traveled over them for more than 300 leagues … with no more landmarks than if we had been swallowed up by the sea …."

When the town was platted in 1903, the five commissioners named it Lamesa, from *la mesa*, Spanish for "the table."

My home county was once part of the vast Long S Ranch, with an estimated 1.3 million acres controlled by C. C. Slaughter, the "Cattle King of Texas." The ranch encompassed an area from Big Spring to Plainview to the New Mexico border. Along with Captain Charles Goodnight, Slaughter helped "rescue" Cynthia Ann Parker, Quanah's mother, who was kidnapped as a child by the Comanches. She would die after being returned to her white relatives, some say of a broken spirit, having become a Comanche herself.

At one time, this part of Texas was a vast grassland home to thousands of buffalo. One of the methods employed by the white man to destroy the feared Comanche was to exterminate the buffalo, the Indians' primary source of food, clothing, and shelter. Buffalo hides were valuable. The buffalo hunters came into West Texas slaughtering as many as a thousand a day.

The extinction began in 1874, the same year the United States Army commenced the Red River Wars to subdue the Comanche. By the late 1800s, the buffalo and the Comanche had disappeared from the South Plains.

In 1901, the Texas Supreme Court ruled that ranchers could no longer renew their ranch leases on the vast South Plains. The state lands had to be sold to the public, a requirement that proved to be the demise of the Long S Ranch. Soon, farmers migrated to Dawson County for cheap land. Over the next thirty years, the once rich grassland became tilled farms raising cotton. By the 1930s, the one-time buffalo grazing haven became the source of terrible sandstorms, part of the aptly named "Dust Bowl" of the '30s era. And this is where my parents, Tom and Florence Conner, settled in 1944.

Dad had been a traveling auditor for Texaco. Headquartered in Dallas, he worked up and down the East Coast. Mom was beautiful. Dad was instantly attracted to this petite, brown-haired, blue-eyed girl. His eyes drew to her every day in Dallas as she waited for her bus. How Dad managed to meet her, I don't know. Suffice it to say they were married in Savannah, Georgia, in 1941, the site of Dad's latest workplace.

Knowing that they needed to put down roots, Dad asked Texaco to assign him the next available bulk plant that wholesaled its products. That turned out to be in Lamesa.

After arriving in Lamesa, they bought farmland, tilled for cotton, and built a house that sat fifty yards off the highway. Dad sharecropped the land with our neighbor, Mr. Scott. While Dad provided the fields, Mr. Scott was responsible for the labor and cottonseed. They split the profits.

Mom was from Anson, Texas, some 120 miles west of Lamesa. Born in 1921, she was the youngest of seven children. Her parents settled in Anson in 1893, having come from Wedowee, Alabama. This part of Dixie was still suffering even though the Civil War had been over for twenty-eight years. Cheap land in Texas beckoned.

Pioneers headed west, always thinking that rain would follow. It didn't. Mom vouched for this. As a young girl, she would go on evening walks with her father. Looking up at clouds, he would say, "Florence Ann, I think there's rain in those clouds." But the rain gods were unmerciful. My grandfather, A. S. Reaves, would soon open a general merchandise store on the west side of the square in Anson. He became prominent in the community and was elected tax assessor-collector for Jones County.

When Mom was twelve, her father lost his eyesight. Due to the Depression and the resultant hard times in Anson, Mom moved to Dallas to live with her adult sister, Pearl Annette (whom we all called "Aunt Pal"), and her husband, Don Taylor.

Mom was a talented pianist with a beautiful soprano voice. In her late teens and early twenties, she became a featured soloist at Highland Park Methodist Church in Dallas. The big bands of the 1940s would play in the downtown hotel ballrooms and, many times, she was invited to sing with them. One of the bands offered her a job as lead singer, which would give her the opportunity to travel the country. Aunt Pal would not allow it. After all, Florence was still her baby sister.

Mom's musical talent remained a joy to many throughout her life. She sang in church choirs and community bands, most notably the Slumtown Symfunny, a group founded by Richard Crawley, the Lamesa town banker and a musician at heart. This group was comprised of talented Lamesa musicians, and she was its featured singer.

Richard was a fascinating man. He graduated from the Cincinnati Conservatory of Music, where the famous New Orleans trumpet player Al Hirt played second chair to him. During World War II, Richard played trumpet in General Patton's Band in North Africa and Europe.

The Symfunny he assembled played—and Florence sang—for events all over West Texas for many years. One of her favorite songs was "On a Clear Day You Can See Forever." When she died at age ninety-four, it was sung at her funeral.

Dad was born in 1906 in Roane, Texas, a small farming community near Corsicana, sixty miles south of Dallas. His grandfather, the first Thomas Conner, came to Texas in 1853 from the Illinois coal mines. Farming in the black land of East Texas was more appealing than mining for black coal.

Like Mom, Dad was the youngest of seven children. In his teens, the family moved to nearby Corsicana, where my grandfather William was a merchant. Like most small Texas towns in those days, Corsicana seemingly had a church on every corner. When Dad was a boy, a large parade was held in support of Prohibition. An elegant convertible came down the street with some town lovelies on board. When my grandfather chuckled, Dad asked him what was funny. Grandfather pointed to the car's driver and said, "Son, that's the biggest bootlegger in town."

Grandfather William had varied careers in his life. He was also the superintendent of the state orphanage in Corsicana. He remarked one day, "There's a real smart boy we have. I think he will go far one day." The boy was Joe Greenhill. He would become the Chief Justice of the Texas Supreme Court.

One of my grandfather's most significant accomplishments was his service on the commission to develop Fair Park in Dallas for the 1936 Centennial of the State of Texas. Its art deco buildings are still in use and admired today as the site of the annual State Fair of Texas.

Dad left Corsicana for Austin to attend the University of Texas, becoming the first in his family to attend college. He graduated with a business degree in 1927.

Fresh out of college, his first job was with Texas Power and Light, the main electricity provider in Texas. None of his bosses had been to college, and they were skeptical of this college boy. To put him in his place, they made him a lineman, climbing poles to repair electric lines. He must have gained their confidence because soon he was assigned a more exciting task—designing an electric cable to cross the Brazos River at Waco.

One of the more peculiar stories from his time with the power company came when electricity was extended into rural Texas. One of Dad's jobs was to determine the placement of power lines based on population. On one such mission, he accompanied a local farmer in his horse-drawn wagon, up and down the country roads. The farmer told Dad the number of people living in the houses, the number of children under their roofs, and other demographic information about the area. Dad kept noticing that many farmhouses had a small house next to the main house. The farmer told him they were "weaning houses." The obvious question followed: "What's a weaning house?" The farmer explained that most of the farm girls had never been away from their mothers. So when they were first married, the new couple would visit and stay in the weaning house.

Texas Power and Light found itself in direct competition with Brown and Root, which wanted to dam the rivers above Austin to create rural electrification. Dad was assigned the job of trying to deter this project. The most prominent proponent for Brown and Root was a young congressman named Lyndon Johnson. Dad and LBJ would often debate the pros and cons of their respective electrification plans on courthouse squares throughout Central Texas. Years later, President Johnson wrote Dad, "In spite of our differences, you are one of the finest men I know." Unfortunately, that letter was lost in one of Mom's several moves. In my mind's eye I can still see it framed over Dad's desk.

Dad was a tinkerer. He learned Morse code as a young boy and built his own radio. In his teens, he became an amateur radio operator, commonly called a "ham." Before instant communication—even before there was good telephone service—ham operators would talk worldwide. They still do. Required to be licensed by the FCC, Dad received his call letters, W5UIJ, *Whiskey Five Uncle Item Jig* in ham parlance.

Not only did he have a radio set at our home, but he also had one of the first mobile ham radios in his car. He was part of MARS, the Military Affiliate Radio System, sponsored by the Department of Defense. The government would ask hams to do special projects. One stands out in my memory.

In 1947, a flying disc crashed in Roswell, New Mexico, some 170 miles west of Lamesa, creating worldwide headlines about UFOs. For several years after that, hams were charged with looking for UFOs. I vividly remember being a young boy, riding with Dad at night in his car. The incredibly bright stars were shining in the clear West Texas sky. My wide-awake eyes scanned the skies for UFOs. The memories of that remain—those bright stars in the brilliantly clear West Texas sky.

3

Moving On

WE LIVED IN THE COUNTRY UNTIL I was in the second grade, when my parents sold the farmhouse with plans to build a new home in town. We moved to a rental house they owned at 414 Terrace Circle in Park Terrace. Before they could finalize the plans for our new home, Mom was diagnosed with colon cancer. Being so young, I failed to realize what a dangerous disease she had. There was a concerted effort on my parents' part to shield me from the reality of Mom's condition.

Her brother, A. S. Reaves, Jr.—"Uncle Mike"—was the administrator at Jefferson Davis Hospital, the county-funded charity hospital in Houston, and well known in the Texas Medical Center. Uncle Mike and the world-famous heart surgeon Dr. Michael DeBakey pioneered the program to have Baylor Medical School residents work at Jeff Davis, a win-win for the hospital and the medical school. As a result of this friendship, Uncle Mike was able to get the finest cancer doctors in the Texas Medical Center to care for Mom. Because we would be there for weeks, it was decided I would live with Dad's brother—Uncle Jack—and his wife, Aunt Bessie.

Bessie was a remarkable woman from Mississippi who taught first grade. Her father was a doctor. In the early 1900s, he reputedly amassed the state's largest private library. Bessie went to Columbia University in New York for her master's degree. It was the '30s, a time when it was rare for women to attend college. Had Bessie lived in the modern era, she probably would have been a high-powered executive or professional.

Uncle Jack was in the wholesale grocery business. As a young man, he joined the army and served in France in World War I. Before he departed for Europe, my grandfather had a family photograph taken. Grandfather believed they would never see Jack again. Fortunately, upon his arrival in France, the army discovered he was one of the few soldiers who could drive a car. In their wisdom, they assigned him to drive officers' cars, so he avoided the terrible bloodshed of trench warfare.

The time I spent in Houston is lost to me, due to my young age. But good news emerged. Mom's colon cancer surgery was successful. We returned to Lamesa. I recall the neighborhood kids being glad to see me, and I was glad to see them. Nothing had changed on Terrace Circle.

In 1959, Dad sold the Texaco business and we moved to Houston, a surprise to me. As part of the move, Dad became the Midwest manager of Ford Gum and Machine Company of Akron, New York. Local civic organizations such as the Lions Club sponsored Ford's penny gumball machines. The club members solicited permission from shop owners to place the gumball machines in their stores. They were very popular among kids with pennies to spend on a little round ball of chewing gum.

On one of Dad's work trips, he became acquainted with Dr. Lloyd Davis, future first lady Nancy Reagan's father, who lived in Phoenix, Arizona. How the connection was made is unknown. Dad knew that Ronald and Nancy Reagan were in Phoenix at Dr. Davis's home while Dad was there on business. The future president was a movie star at the time, best known as the host of the TV series *The General Electric Theater*.

Dad called the Davis home and spoke with Reagan, asking him to make a public service announcement for Ford Gum. Dad said Reagan was friendly and gracious, inviting him to his in-laws' home. With Dad's portable tape recorder, a new gadget at the time, Reagan voiced a radio ad for Ford Gum. The tape and script are gone, but I recall Reagan saying, "Chew for charity."

The Houston move was disquieting for me, and the first few weeks of sixth grade were stressful, meeting new kids and making friends. Over several months, the adage "time takes care of everything" proved true. Houston and I were doing just fine.

Our house was located at 2214 MacArthur, a stone's throw from the magnificent Shamrock Hilton Hotel and the Texas Medical Center. From my second-floor bedroom window at night, I admired this magnificent hotel, its brightly lit rooms and the large green neon sign atop the building that proclaimed "The Shamrock Hilton."

It was not the only sight from my bedroom. Across Main Street, the twenty-story Prudential Life Insurance building's top three floors had a bright neon sign illuminating a large mountain jutting into the sea, a reminder that this company was "As Strong as the Rock of Gibraltar."

The Shamrock was built in 1949 by the legendary Glenn McCarthy, a hard charger, gambler, drinker, and wildcatter, the inspiration for the character Jett Rink in Edna Ferber's *Giant*. Its green-tiled roof covered eighteen stories. The Shamrock presided over South Main like the Colossus of Rhodes. Its Olympic-sized swimming pool was so large that McCarthy launched a boat in it, with beautiful girls waterskiing around its perimeter to the delight of hotel guests.

In 1955, only six years after McCarthy built the hotel, the Hilton chain acquired it. In 1985, the hotel was no longer profitable. Hilton donated the property to the Texas Medical Center. The famous structure was demolished two years later. An old man, having lost several fortunes, watched as this magnificent building was reduced to rubble. He was Glenn McCarthy.

4

My First Job

WE LIVED IN HOUSTON FROM MY SIXTH through ninth grades. I attended Lanier Junior High, whose alumni include renowned CBS anchorman Walter Cronkite, famed heart surgeon pioneer Dr. Denton Cooley, and Texas governor Mark White.

The present I received for my thirteenth birthday is long forgotten, but I remember Dad's words. No more "walking around money" from him. I needed to get a job for drug store soft drinks, movie tickets, and trinkets. This was news. I had never thought about a job.

At that time, Houston had two major daily newspapers: the morning *Houston Post* and the afternoon *Houston Chronicle*. There was also a third paper, the afternoon *Houston Press*. It was much smaller than the others and did not publish on Sunday.

The *Press* was known for tawdry, brash stories about violence and sex. One of its notorious stories, lasting for days, headlined the woman who boarded crowded city buses, then punched men's backs with her steel-pointed bra. One *Press* reporter commented that it was "a paper that, by journalistic standards, had no standards at all."

Its most famous columnist was Maxine Messinger, also known as Miss Moonlight. Her writing was described as "1940s highball." She coined such terms as "swankienda," "slow down for the low down," and "playcation." She would write about the town's rich and famous, their hijinks and foibles. The readers loved it.

In those days, a paper route was a great first job for a young enterprising kid. It was a small business in a microcosm. You bought your product from the paper, delivered it to the customers, collected the money from them, paid for your papers, and kept the profit. The only available *Press* route close to me was the south side of Rice Village, the first suburban shopping center in Houston. With only twenty-seven subscribers, I needed to grow my route. Going door to door, I solicited new subscriptions.

The homeowners on my route couldn't miss my bike, its *Houston Press* bags covering the back wheel like saddlebags, nor me, a chubby little kid with hands covered in newsprint, asking for their business. I soon realized good marketing with phrases like, "It's only a $1.45 a month" and "If you like, I'll put it on your front porch or by your back door." If the lady of the house answered the door, I could usually close the deal. I was successful enough that the route manager, a gawky-looking guy who drove a white Volvo, gave me a larger route that encompassed the streets behind the Shamrock Hilton.

Sakowitz was the most elegant department store in Houston at that time. One of the Sakowitz brothers lived in the penthouse atop the hotel. My last stop was delivering his paper to the Shamrock's bell captain, who would then deliver it to Mr. Sakowitz. It always puzzled me why a bellboy didn't bring the paper from the hotel newsstand, a mystery unsolved to this day.

In 1961, Hurricane Carla hit Galveston. She was no lady. A category five storm of the ages, she roared up the Gulf Freeway to Houston. I called my route manager to see if paperboys got a reprieve. No. He delivered our bundled papers to us as usual. As the eye of the storm passed over, I faithfully biked my rounds. While this sounds crazy—and frankly, it was—a rain-soaked paperboy dutifully completed his rounds. Coming from windswept West Texas, Mom and I commented that a hurricane was like a sandstorm, but wet.

On Saturdays, my friends and I would typically catch the bus to head downtown. Our routine was predictable. We would go to Oshman's Sporting Goods on Main, then to Archie's Fun Shop for magic paraphernalia. Then hot dogs at James Coney Island and a movie at the Majestic or Metropolitan. In the '70s, most of the downtown stores relocated to the suburbs. Eventually these grand old downtown movie palaces fell victim to the wrecking ball.

An additional bonus was in store for me living in Houston close to my aunt and uncle, Bessie and Jack. I was horse-crazy from the time I was a little boy. My childhood heroes were Roy Rogers, Gene Autry, and the Cisco Kid. My favorite footwear was boots. In my imagination, I was the best cowboy and gunslinger in the Old West. I needed a horse.

To my good fortune, Uncle Jack thought it was an excellent idea for the two of us to get horses. The Almeda Stables abutted Hermann Park near the Medical Center. When Mr. Hermann bequeathed the park in 1914, he insisted that it have a bridle path.

In the evening, Uncle Jack would pick me up to go to the stables. Saddling up, we rode through the park, my uncle on his gelding, Prince, me on my bay mare, Dixie. The large live oak trees that shaded the park were draped in Spanish moss. I have a clear recollection of looking through my horse's twitching ears down on now familiar trails.

The Houston Fat Stock Show and Rodeo came to town in February of each year. The stable's owner organized a group to ride in the rodeo parade in 1963. Jack and I got to the stables just as the sun rose in the east. Saddling our horses as they nickered in the cool air, we formed our group and rode the city streets into the downtown, joining the Houston Rodeo Parade.

The now-called Houston Livestock Show and Rodeo was and still is the largest annual event in the city. At that time, schools were dismissed for Go Texan Day, the first Friday of the rodeo. Children and adults crowded the streets for the parade. In my imagination, I was an important young cowboy, waving my hat and flashing my spurs to the packed crowds along Main Street. Little did I know that would be the first of many Houston Rodeo parades for me. I would become a show director and ride in the parade for many years.

The Almeda Stables closed, and we moved our horses to the Shamrock Stables on Fannin Street, south of the medical center. There were no riding paths, so we would ride a few blocks down Fannin to Braes Bayou. We rode along its banks or perhaps on a large, vacant piece of land further south. Construction crews were excavating a large hole in the ground. After the workers left for the day, Jack and I would ride around this site, looking down this ever-deepening hole. This would become the Astrodome.

My days in Houston were an introduction to the city where I would spend my adulthood. But in 1962, Dad and a partner purchased the Lamesa radio station. By 1963, Dad and Mom had decided it was time to go home.

5

Return to West Texas

RETURNING TO LAMESA WAS A SOURCE OF some anxiety. I was now a Houstonian being reclaimed by a small West Texas town. I left as a child. I returned a teenager.

Some of my Lamesa contemporaries from my childhood now viewed me as a city boy. One comment on my return was, "You talk funny." Four years in Houston cured much of my West Texas twang. Soon enough, I reconnected with old friends and made new ones.

An important person during those years was Kathy Crawley, the daughter of the Slumtown Symfunny's trumpet-playing banker, who took a shine to me. I was smitten with her as well. She was cute, popular, and a cheerleader. She always wore a smile and had something positive to say to everyone. I called her "Sunshine."

One of our high school traditions was circling the courthouse square in our cars. The boys would drive clockwise on the inside, the girls counterclockwise on the outside. When we saw a carload of girls we wanted to connect with, we'd yell, "Meet us at Wall!"

The Wall was a two-story brick wall on the backside of Higginbotham's lumberyard, one block south of the square. To this day, high school kids paint their names or the names of their girlfriends on the wall. They also resort to renderings of the Lamesa High School mascot, the Golden Tornado, or harmless graffiti. For my part, I painted Kathy's name on the Wall. That contribution and countless others have been painted over many times. Artists travel to Lamesa to paint the Wall, including Dick Wray, a prominent Houston artist who would later become a client of mine.

High school meant Friday night football, the Methodist Youth Fellowship, the Sky Vue drive-in theater, A&W Root Beer, and Leon's Drive-Ins for burgers and Cokes. There also were the trips to Lubbock for first-run movies, and "parking" in the roads abutting the cotton fields

I got my first vehicle in 1964, a 1952 Ford pickup. It was a bargain at $250. The odometer and the heater had long since died. A hole in the floor allowed the cold West Texas wind to penetrate the cab in the winter. It had a small engine and three-speed manual transmission, and its original green paint had faded to a dull grayish green.

For the homecoming parade in 1965, the cheerleaders decided that riding in the back of my truck would be an eye-catcher. Using white liquid shoe polish, they wrote slogans on its side in large letters. Among them were "Go Tors!" and "Give 'em Hell!" Waving from the old pickup bed in their cheerleading outfits, the pretty girls and the old truck were a huge hit. After the parade, we washed the truck. Off came the shoe polish. Miraculously, where the polish was removed, the aged patina of the faded paint gave way to dark green. Now the slogans appeared on the truck in their new shade. After that, my truck was known as "Give 'em."

Students in the 1960s were fortunate. We had exceptional women teachers. Had they been born thirty years later, they would have been doctors, lawyers, scientists, and business executives. But these women grew up in an era when teaching was one of the few acceptable professions for women.

My senior English teacher, Lucille Ogletree, was the perfect example. She was the best teacher I ever had. Not only did we learn about subjective and objective adjectives, participles, and sentence construction, but she also taught us how to write. *When writing a thank you note after thanking the person for the gift, always include a personal note. Far more important than the gift, your gift of friendship will be cherished forever.* I still write my "thank-yous" using Lucille's instructions.

She wanted us to excel. The University Interscholastic League provided competition among Texas schools in debate and public speaking. Lucille chose me for declamation and, as she did for other students, she spent hours after school coaching me. For my speech, she chose General Douglas MacArthur's speech to the West Point cadets, "Duty, Honor, Country." To this day, I can recite most of it.

She received no additional compensation for her afterschool hours with her students. She did these things because she loved us. She loved teaching. She loved watching us grow and flourish. This great teacher was thin and angular, her salt and pepper hair pulled back in a bun with a pencil sticking out at ear level. I see her to this day, clutching a stack of student essays, taking them home to grade.

Spring has always been an important time for high school seniors. My graduating class in 1966 was less than two hundred people. We were a diverse group of whites, Hispanics, Blacks, farm boys and girls, and townies. We came from across the socio-economic strata. Many would go only as far as high school. Most college-bound students went to Texas Tech, a smattering to TCU and Baylor, and some to junior college. And, indeed, some of us would eventually graduate from "The University," our speak for the University of Texas.

High school was over. I was off to the next adventure—in Austin. But next, I digress to one of the most fun things I've ever done.

6

The Radio Years

THE TOWN OF BIG SPRING GOT ITS name from a single large spring that issued into a small gorge at the base of Scenic Mountain, southwest of the city. It was a watering hole for Apaches, Comanches, and buffalo hunters. Located at the intersection of US Highway 180 and Interstate 20, Big Spring is a major crossroads in West Texas.

In 1959, Dad and his friend Bob Bradbury purchased a radio station. The studios of KHEM were in the basement of the Settles Hotel. Built in 1930, it was the tallest building between Fort Worth and El Paso. It still is. To a twelve-year-old, the lobby was grand, with its large staircase and three-story vaulted ceilings. In the 1970s, the hotel fell into disrepair. In 2006, Briant Ryan, a Dallas owner of an international accounting firm and Big Spring native, invested $30 million to update and refurbish it into a luxury hotel.

Back in our day, anyone entering the lobby was greeted by a neon sign above a stairway, brightly announcing the call letters KHEM. Downstairs, there were cramped rooms and a small studio. There were no tape recorders then. Records were played and the announcers would broadcast everything live. Dad's partner Bob would joke that he sold ads for "a dollar a holler," and he would hire anyone who could read as a radio announcer.

By 1961, the partners had built a new broadcast facility just east of town, nestled against the south side of Interstate 20. The station played country music, except from 9 a.m. to noon. That time belonged to Mr. Sunshine. He played gospel music, and, tapping a small xylophone, in his sing-song voice, he intoned, "Welcome to the Sunshine Hour!"

Sunshine had a tremendous following. The programming would be considered corny today, but many West Texans of the '60s loved it. In the movie *Midnight Cowboy*, Jon Voight's character, Joe Buck, is leaving Big Spring for New York. On the Greyhound bus, he is listening to his transistor radio—to Mr. Sunshine.

In 1962, the partners purchased KPET in Lamesa. A year later, we returned there so Dad could manage that station. Within another year, Dad and Bob parted on amicable terms. Bob took KHEM and Dad KPET.

The station was community oriented. All small Texas towns revolved around their high school, primarily the football team and whatever else the students were involved in. KPET broadcast all high school football, basketball, and baseball games, as well as the hospital admissions and discharges, obituaries, and even live remote spots from car dealerships, introducing the new models. Church services filled a lot of the airtime. Lamesa relied on KPET for local news: police reports, farm reports, civic club meetings, and actions of the city council.

While the larger stations in Lubbock and Midland had more sophisticated programming, when you walked into a store in Lamesa or pulled up next to a car playing a radio, you heard KPET.

Just before my sixteenth birthday in 1964, I got my shot at being a radio disc jockey. Because Dad owned KPET, getting hired was not a steep hill to climb. I hosted the Bennett Ford Sales Country Music Show from 4 to 6 p.m. every Saturday, Top 40 radio until sign-off at 10, then Sundays from 2 p.m. to sign off. I loved it. I would also fill in for vacationing DJs in other time slots.

My only brush with the law came one night in the company of a young DJ working at KPET. Aubrey Cook would later become a top jock at KONO in San Antonio, changing his DJ name to Nick St. John. He was in his early twenties, from Dallas, and we clicked. Dawson County was dry. The closest place to buy alcohol was Big Spring, forty-five miles south of Lamesa. Aubrey could not fathom living in a town where you couldn't buy a beer, much less that there were virtually no women his age to date. Unable to solve his dating dilemma, I could at least help with the beer.

Big Momma was a large Black lady who lived in the Flat, a segregated area on the east side of town. She had a shotgun shack with a large living room and kitchen area. At the back of the room was an old white refrigerator filled with quart bottles of Schlitz beer. Big Momma charged a dollar a bottle. Aubrey and I bought our beers and went to a cotton field turnrow, a dirt path where the tractors turn when plowing. We parked the car and cracked open Milwaukee's finest. No more than two minutes had passed when out of the darkness, flashing police lights appeared behind us.

An officer of the law approached our car, shining his flashlight on our faces. Faster than you can say Miranda rights, we were at the Lamesa Police Department. My worst fear was that Dad would find out. Aubrey's worst fear was that he would go to prison for contributing to the delinquency of a minor. I was sixteen years old. I was able to get home at a decent hour and kept my night's adventure to myself. The following week, we were invited to see District Attorney Vernon Adcock.

Like all small towns, everyone knew everyone else. I was contrite. I told Mr. Adcock that I was very sorry. I made a mistake. As Aubrey's young life flashed before him, I told Mr. Adcock that Aubrey had not led me down this path of degradation. More likely it was the reverse. The DA was understanding. He told us to go and not make the same mistake again. I commented to him that Dad did not know of my introduction to the Lamesa Police Station. On leaving his office, he commented, "Don't worry, Tommy. I won't tell him."

This was one item that was never mentioned on KPET's local news.

Being a DJ proved to be popular with the high school crowd. During the mid-60s, a famous San Francisco nightclub called the Whiskey a Go-Go featured girls in short skirts and white go-go boots. They would dance in cages above the audience. There was also a TV show called *Hullabaloo* that featured go-go dancers. Latching onto the "go-go" craze, on the radio, I called myself "TC a Go-Go."

For many years, when seeing former classmates, they still said, "Hey, Go-Go." To this day, people call me TC. Because of my radio exposure, I was asked to emcee events at the high school and church, and I always took every opportunity to DJ at the station.

On November 22, 1963, several of us left high school for lunch at one of the fast-food drive-ins. Returning to school, the radio announcer broke in with a news bulletin from Dallas. The president had been shot. I raced to KPET and stood over the Associated Press wire service machine as it typed with its usual clatter the fateful news out of Dallas.

The final report came in the early afternoon. President John F. Kennedy was dead. There was dead silence among us at the station. The DJ on duty, without prompting from anyone, began to play somber hymn music. Like the nation, Lamesa, including its teenaged disc jockey, was shocked to the core.

Years later, I became friends with Dr. Robert Grossman, head of the Department of Neurology at Houston's Baylor College of Medicine. On that fateful day, he was a resident at Parkland Hospital. While the senior surgeons were futilely trying to save the president's life, Dr. Grossman told me his role that day was holding Kennedy's brains in the back of his head. There was a thought that would never escape him. As he looked down on the face known to millions, he thought, "What a handsome young man."

Like any radio or TV station, KPET's income was from advertising. Taking advantage of the large Hispanic population market, KPET had a Hispanic announcer, Ray Gonzalez. Ray would sell his ads and ad lib them between Mexican records, now called Tejano music. Ray was an entrepreneur. He would sell personalized greetings for special events like Mother's Day. His wife would sit at the station's front door as a long line of cars pulled up and sons, daughters, and grandchildren paid for their special greetings.

Dawson County sits at the southern end of Tornado Alley, which extends north to South Dakota. During the spring, the changing weather spawns tornados. The late '60s did not enjoy sophisticated weather forecasting and high-tech radar. We relied on visual sightings, the only precise way to track these violent twisters. If a farmer or someone in town spied a tornado, he would call the sheriff's office or the police department. Deputies and officers would patrol, looking for tornados, radioing back to the dispatcher the twister's location and movement. In severe weather situations, we were on the air giving tornado locations and warning our listeners to take cover out of harm's way.

It was a Saturday afternoon in the spring of 1965. The sky was dark. The wind was picking up, whistling. The lightning punched through menacing, dark clouds. Thunder roared. The old-timers knew what this meant: tornadoes.

I was working the Saturday afternoon shift at KPET. The sheriff's dispatcher called me. "Tommy, we've got two tornadoes on the ground, west of town." Immediately I patched him in to broadcast live on the air. This was followed shortly by the Lamesa police dispatcher.

We were live with reports from the officers as they tracked the tornadoes. The folks with storm cellars sheltered in them. The First National Bank opened its basement for employees and their families. This weather threat was the real deal. I knew the entire town was listening to—and relying on—KPET.

The storms passed. Four confirmed tornadoes would wind up only causing minor damage. After several hours of tense broadcasting, I finally relaxed. Only then did I realize that during this emergency, I was alone at the radio station, with no windows, at the top of a hill. Had a tornado touched down nearby, I would have had no way of knowing. I was sixteen years old.

7

The Big Stick

IT WAS THE SUMMER OF 1967 BETWEEN my freshman and sophomore years at UT. Dad had business in Houston that would keep him there for a while, so my folks rented an apartment. I went with them because I had an idea. What if I could land a DJ job in the largest radio market in Texas?

My sights were not set on one of the top stations. I thought I might find a spot at one of the FM stations. AM was the place to be. Top 40 Radio was at its peak. FM stations played classical and waiting room music.

The first station I tried was KQUE FM. It played gentle, middle-of-the-road music. Webb Hunt was the program director, and a nice guy. Armed with my demo tape from KPET, he politely listened and said, "Your voice is too young for KQUE. Why don't you go next door to KNUZ?"

KNUZ AM was the number-two rated station in the Bayou City market, promoted as "The Big Stick." The morning DJ was the legendary Paul Berlin, who at one time was the highest-paid DJ in the country.

With no appointment, I told the receptionist why I was there. "Could I see the program director?"

Within minutes, I was in Buddy McGregor's office. A handsome guy with slicked-back black hair, Buddy proudly displayed a large picture of himself seated with the Beatles. Buddy was the first American DJ to go to England and interview them. I thought to myself, "This is the big time."

I also noticed that Buddy was frazzled. He listened to my tape audition perfunctorily. I was in the right place at the right time. The 7 p.m.-to-midnight jock had walked out an hour before I walked in. With no notice, he quit. The midnight-to-6 a.m. DJ would be taking his place. Buddy desperately needed someone to pull the graveyard shift.

Barely pausing, Buddy asked, "Can you start tonight?"

In my mind, I yelled to myself, "No problem, Buddy!"

I returned to the station at 8 that night. Dave Watts, the newly promoted 7-to-midnight jock, taught me the "board" and the format. The board is a piece of broadcast equipment. Three feet long, it has a series of dials controlling each output: the DJ's mic, turntables, commercials, jingles, and the newsroom mic. All the records, commercials, announcements, jingles—all had to meld flawlessly with no dead air. This was the way radio was done. I learned that on the hill in Lamesa. Thankfully, the KNUZ board was much like the one at KPET. I mastered it with no problem.

The next thing to learn was the format: what happens when. Five minutes of news at the top of the hour, weather at fifteen past the hour, headlines at the half-hour, sports at fifteen till. After the top-of-the-hour news, the newsman would intone, "This is David Fowler for KNUZ News, heard at the top of every hour. For KNUZ music, it's Good Guy Tom Conner!" All KNUZ jocks were known as Good Guys. It was used in all the station promotions.

When my shift ended at 6 a.m., I had been without sleep for almost twenty-four hours. I was still wide awake. This was big-city radio. I had just pulled a shift as the newest KNUZ Good Guy. Following me was the famous DJ Paul Berlin. He was about to walk in the door.

Throughout the five minutes of the 6 a.m. news, I kept waiting for Berlin, but no Berlin appeared.

The news was over. In a baritone voice, Fowler announced, "… and for KNUZ Music, it's Good Guy Paul Berlin!"

No Berlin. I did what I was taught to do: I hit a Top 10 record.

This was morning drive time. This was the number one market in Texas. Where was the station's number one DJ? About sixty seconds into the song, Berlin walked in. Nice guy. We shook hands and he sat down and casually began his typical friendly chatter with the audience.

Berlin's habit for years was to have breakfast at One's A Meal, a twenty-four-hour restaurant near the station. While there, he would read the morning *Houston Post* and get ideas for show patter. His timing was perfect both on and off the air. He knew exactly when to leave for the station to arrive *just* before the newest Good Guy imploded. Berlin did this every morning when I worked the graveyard shift.

1967 was the Summer of Love. The Beatles released *Sergeant Pepper's Lonely Hearts Club Band*. The Doors released their first big hit, "Light My Fire." A Mississippi girl came to Houston promoting her new record. Buddy took her to lunch. The following week, Bobbie Gentry's "Ode to Billie Joe" was the number one song on KNUZ.

1967 also was the year of the race riots. Despite President Johnson's landmark civil rights legislation, poverty, police injustice, joblessness, and other problems for Black people lit the tinderbox of violence. Houston was not spared. In May of that year, a riot at the predominately Black Texas Southern University ended with the death of a Houston police officer. A couple of months later, another riot broke out at the University of Houston.

That summer night, the police scanner lit up the newsroom. Police cars were being summoned from all across Houston. My newsman squawked on the intercom. He was headed to the university. The KNUZ studios were less than two and a half miles from the campus. The studios were in a large converted two-story home that backed up to a parking lot. A large double-paned glass window separated the newsroom and the control room where I sat.

Like the afternoon of the tornadoes a few years earlier, I was alone in the station. It was 2 a.m., so it was nerve-racking when I looked up and saw a Black man staring at me from the newsroom. In his haste, my newsman had left the back door open. The stranger appeared middle-aged. With a race riot going on a couple of miles away, my heart raced. Entering the newsroom, I told him that no one was allowed in the station, that my night manager would soon return, and I would get in trouble if the he was still there. Of course, there was no night manager, but my mind was in high gear, searching for excuses to get this man out. I lightly touched his back and moved toward the open door. He didn't resist and calmly walked out, never saying a word. Shutting the door, I slammed every lock in place.

Fall was fast approaching. I dutifully notified McGregor that I was headed to UT. By this time, I had been promoted to the 7-to-midnight shift. Thanks to some good coaching from the KNUZ pros, my on-air abilities had improved. I was a major market disc jockey.

Arriving at UT, I made an appointment with Jeff Stevens, the program director at KNOW, Austin's number one station. With a 51 percent share of the market, it enjoyed unheard-of ratings in a multi-station market.

I took my demo tape from KNUZ. When I told Jeff I had worked there, he went to another office for a quick phone call. My guess is that he called McGregor. When he returned, I had a job. The KNUZ connection was strong.

I was a full-time student, so I started doing weekend shifts. Within weeks, I was the permanent fill-in DJ, the go-to guy if another jock was sick or on vacation. Morning drive, afternoon drive, it made no difference. I worked them all, and I worked with several DJs and newsmen who would later enter the Texas Radio Hall of Fame: Paul Berlin, Joe Ford, Jay Allen, and Jim Ray, to name a few. The morning jock was Ed Brandon, who would become the long-tenured weatherman at KTRK TV Channel 13 in Houston.

Getting a DJ job at Austin's number one station was also great for my student life at the University of Texas.

8

The University

ARRIVING AT THE UNIVERSITY OF TEXAS, I had no immediate plans to join a fraternity. A good friend from Amarillo, Mel Phillips, had been active in DeMolay politics and now fancied himself a college political kingmaker. In a sense, he was.

The Representative Party was a campus political organization comprising members from each fraternity. Its support of a candidate was almost a guarantee for the election of the student body president and student senate members. Mel was chairman of this group and a member of Phi Kappa Psi. And I became a Phi Psi pledge in no time.

The Phi Psi house, at 2801 Longview, was ten blocks from campus, a one-story building with the main living room, dining room, and kitchen in the center and wings off to each side for the living quarters. There was a basement where chapter meetings were held. There also was a small office for the president and officers.

Pledging consisted of being subservient to the brothers, learning their names and hometowns and the Phi Psi ritual. None of this was complicated. At the end of your pledge semester was

Hell Week. Most of it was stupid. The most memorable event that I care to recount was having to stand on a chair blindfolded and being told to jump off onto tacks on the floor, which were just crushed ice. After much sleep deprivation, at the end of the week you were initiated into the brotherhood. I have always viewed this behavior as childish and stupid. If you want to be a friend and brother to someone, why would you degrade them?

I became the president of my chapter in my senior year. My first order of business: abolish Hell Week. I created "Work Week" in its place. We determined repairs, painting, and other house needs for the pledges to handle. No hazing was allowed. The following year, the new brothers—who had not gone through Hell Week—reinstituted it—a prime example of the maturity of young men.

Being president had its challenges. One was money. We were short of cash. One of the perks of being in a fraternity was having a place to live with friends with reasonable rent, but sometimes the rental income fell short of our budgetary needs.

The air conditioner went out in April. Although Austin was lovely in the spring, it was getting warmer with each passing day. The lads were beginning to complain. The problem: We did not have the money to fix the AC. Before I had a full-scale mutiny, I came up with an excuse. The parts for the AC were coming from Japan—on a boat—which was why it was taking so long. To my amazement, the brothers bought that tale. Within a few weeks, we were able to make the repairs.

Our house mother, Mrs. Cook, lived on the premises in her private quarters, as did all house mothers of that period. Mrs. Cook's primary duties were to manage the kitchen and its help. While I complimented her on the food and the job she was doing, I explained to her we were short of money, and she needed to cut expenses. A month passed with no pared-down food bill.

The officers and I were meeting in the basement when I got the news. I sent a pledge upstairs to invite Mrs. Cook to come to the basement. This lady had lived in the house for at least two years, but in that time, she had never set foot in the basement. She knew that was where the meetings were held, where a lot of Hell Week went on, and—in her mind—God knows what else. Maybe we sacrificed house mothers to the fraternal gods there. She was terrified. When she walked into our little office, she had tears in her eyes and was trembling. Feeling sorry for her, I assured her that we all appreciated her. Again, I explained the budget problem. The next month there were substantial savings in the food bill.

And being at Texas was fun! We had parties with live bands many weekends. In addition, there was always some good-natured teasing and hellraising. At UT, we angered other schools' students by simply referring to our school as "The University."

In the fall of 1969, UT won the national championship in football. Coach Darrell Royal was all but deified. Memorial Stadium was later renamed for him.

Underage drinking was rampant (I know, reader, you are mortified at this revelation). One Saturday night at the end of my KNOW shift at midnight, I commandeered the station's news cruiser. It had flashing blue lights on top and—to the drunken eye—resembled a police cruiser. A party was going full blast with a live band at the Phi Psi house. I pulled up in the yard, facing the plate glass windows of the party room with the blue strobes bouncing off the windows.

I waited thirty seconds before I walked into the house. Not a soul could be found. Spilled beer cups were everywhere. The back doors were wide open. The band members had dropped their instruments and evacuated. Everyone had escaped and raced down the alley to the next street. While there was some initial anger directed at me, in a few minutes it was decided that my prank, in frat language of the time, was "good bullshit."

UT student politics was a training ground for future politicians. Several student body presidents became legislators, congressmen, and governors.

Mel Phillips got me involved in the Representative Party. In the spring of 1968, we solidly backed Rostam "Tom" Kavoussi. Tom's family had immigrated from India, making him the first non-Anglo to run for student body president at UT. He was elected in a landslide. Forty-something years later, I was having a detached retina treated. The young resident assisting my doctor introduced himself as Dr. Kavoussi—he was Tom's son.

Round Up was an annual three-day nonstop party weekend in April that would make students from other schools dream of transferring to UT. The festivities included a parade down The Drag, the street abutting the west side of campus. Melinda Hill was chairwoman and picked me to assist in the publicity, primarily because of my radio contacts. Melinda was an incredible woman. An organizer, she later became chairwoman of the board at Hermann Hospital in Houston.

The previous fall, the big movie had been *Bonnie and Clyde,* starring Warren Beatty and Faye Dunaway. One of our brothers was dating a gorgeous blonde, and we had a pledge who was a dead ringer for Michael J. Pollard, the actor who played the duo's sidekick, C. W. Moss. We requisitioned a vintage 1930s automobile, donned clothes of that era, and found some fake machine guns and pistols. Bonnie, Clyde, and their gang entered the parade. It was a big hit.

An unintended consequence of Round Up was an invitation asking me to emcee the UT Sweetheart Ball at the Coliseum on Town Lake. I was paired with another radio personality, April Raines, a UT coed my age. Yes, her real name was Linda April Raines. Her father was a scientist with a sense of humor. She worked at KTBC FM, which played middle-of-the-road contemporary music.

I had never met April, but I had listened to her. She had an incredibly sexy voice and could turn a great phrase. From experience, I expected a woman with a sexy voice to be dead unattractive. I called April to set up a dinner meeting to discuss our upcoming project. I arrived first. Then she walked in. Stunning, she had been a runner-up to Miss Austin the previous year. She was also a poet, a seamstress, an author, and an actress. An incredibly talented young woman.

The ball was a success. Not to boast, but April and I were good. And after the Ball, things progressed. We were together for the remainder of our college days. She became a Phi Psi Little Sister. To no one's surprise, she was named one of the Ten Most Beautiful at UT during our senior year.

In the spring of 1968, Dad came to town for the Texas Association of Broadcasters convention. He invited our state senator, Lubbock's H. J. "Doc" Blanchard, to the annual dinner. When it was over, Dad asked Doc to accompany us to Dad's hotel room for me to conduct an interview.

Dad had a new cassette tape recorder—one of the first available on the market. Doc had never seen one. Dad told the senator we would do an interview, and he would take the tape back to our Lamesa radio station to play on the local news. I asked Doc about various bills and what he was doing in Austin. It was a real softball interview, enabling him to pontificate about all the great things he was doing for the folks back in West Texas. Doc was fascinated with the whole thing. He invited me to see him at the capitol.

I went to his office later that week. Together, we devised a plan for me to do interviews and news features about Doc to forward to the local radio stations in his district, covering a significant portion of West Texas. This resulted in the secretary of the senate building a small broadcast booth with taping facilities in the basement of the capitol. The other senators soon got the idea and had their own versions of the Tom and Doc Show. The whole thing was a huge success and gave me a ringside seat to state government.

My longest and perhaps most interesting day and night in the state senate was when Doc filibustered a bill, speaking continuously for hours to block the passage of a proposed law. I don't recall the details of the bill, but I do recall the night.

The senate was in session. It was close to midnight. An open bar had been set up behind the senate chambers. Lobbyists, reporters, and all types of hangers-on were coming in and out. It was partying in the back and filibustering in the front. It would surprise me if that still happens today.

Early in my work for Doc, I found myself on the senate floor. I heard this stentorian, elegant, articulate voice addressing the chair. I turned and saw a large Black woman, Barbara Jordan from Houston, the first African American elected to the Texas Senate. A lawyer, she would later become a member of the US Congress, captivating the nation in her role on the House Judiciary Committee—the Watergate committee—considering the impeachment of President Richard Nixon.

The session coincided with the retirement of my high school English teacher, Lucille Ogletree, and her husband, Dan, a history teacher. At my request, Doc introduced a senate resolution in their honor. It was impressively framed and printed on parchment paper with the seal of the senate and the lieutenant governor's signature.

In 1969, I made a special trip to Lamesa to attend the retirement party for the Ogletrees, something I would not miss. After other teachers, former students, and dignitaries praised their careers, I read the senate resolution to the assembled guests. I then proudly presented it to Lucille and Dan. The wording of the resolution was moving. There were tears in their eyes. I was proud. I had done a good job writing it—thanks to Lucille.

9

Six Coeds in a VW Bus

AT UT, OLIVER HEARD BECAME ANOTHER OF my closest friends. A visionary and genius, he came to The University at sixteen, to commence joint undergraduate and law degrees. When he finished both at age twenty, and not being twenty-one, he had to get special permission to take the bar exam.

When I met Oliver, he was already practicing law. However, one career was not enough for him.

In the late '60s, flying to Europe was limited to the wealthy and was thus out of reach to most college students. Oliver had the idea of chartering flights to Europe, allowing students to purchase airfare at a low price. Student Travel, Inc. was born. Over several years, hundreds of Texas college students went to Europe on Student Travel charter flights.

Oliver had another idea: the Volkswagen Bus Tour. During the '60s, college girls usually traveled to Europe on highly structured bus tours with guides and, sometimes, chaperones. His idea was for six girls to sightsee Europe in a VW bus, driven by a college boy. For each girl the boy signed up, one-sixth of the trip price was deducted. He would enjoy a free summer in Europe if he filled a bus. And I did. It was the summer of 1969.

Hotels were reserved in specific cities for specific nights. Several buses usually traveled on the same dates to the next destination where our pre-booked hotel was waiting. The girls decided what their bus would do each day. If we were in Paris on the night of July 5th and the next day was Bordeaux, some girls might elect to sleep in. Another bus's girls might decide to leave early and stop in Cognac and have a Cognac on the way. The entire unstructured trip followed this pattern.

The summer of 1969 introduced me to Europe. Taking the Student Travel charter flight, we arrived in London for four days, the beginning of a new education. Landing at Gatwick, we boarded the train to London. The train cars had compartments that were entered from the outside, like the ones Holmes and Dr. Watson traveled in. It was already an adventure.

Going to my first pub in London, I encountered two Black men, impeccably dressed in tweed suits, speaking with English accents. Coming from 1960s still mostly segregated Texas, this was a new experience. These chaps were quite friendly, charming, and sophisticated, offering me samples of the English beers they were drinking. As the Brits would say, "We got on terribly well." Their courteous demeanor could not belie their surprise that they were talking to an honest-to-God Texan, complete with accent. I was a new species for them.

To be sure, London was a culture shock. We drivers, some ten of us, all stayed in one room on the ground floor of what passed for a youth hostel, unlike any place I had experienced. There were holes in some of the glass panes of the windows, stuffed with rags to ward off the early summer chill. I kept waiting for the Luftwaffe to strafe us. The beds were iron bunks. There was a communal sink in the room with the toilet and bath down the hall. As for the faded paint on the walls, what had not peeled off may have dated from Queen Victoria's reign.

With a 1969 college budget, I stopped at a walk-up food shop. My first sandwich was roast beef. Coming from Texas, the brown-tinged shingle had little resemblance to any beef I had ever eaten. The stale bread was swabbed with what passed for mustard. Then, what passed for hamburgers in London? Wimpy's was the UK's interpretation of Burger King. One Wimpy's, and Toto, we're not in Austin anymore.

But what fun! Taking the interminably long, creaking wooden escalators down to the Tube to whisk us to the sites and, more importantly, to see *Hair* with its young actors extolling dope and nudity and song lyrics about sex in all forms. Of course, we danced in the aisles with abandon.

And the pubs. The lagers and ales. Interminable choices! It was the beginning of my venture into continental sophistication. I soon learned that ice-cold beer was only for American palates. I was fast becoming a seasoned European traveler, in less than seventy-two hours.

From London, we took a ferry at Harwich, England, crossing the Channel to the Hook of Holland. Then on to Amsterdam for our buses. I spent two months on the continent, drove countless miles, and had countless wonderous experiences.

Ann, Christine, Jan, Margot, Mary Jo, and Margaret were all cute UT coeds, and they were nice and good sports. They took turns navigating and changing out the cassette tapes to something other than *Hair*. When we arrived at the hotel, my job was to check everyone in and get our keys. While I did that, they brought their bags in along with mine. Many times, when I got to my room, my luggage was already there. In the bathroom, there might be a freshly drawn bubble bath (still a treat to me) and a glass of red wine on the side of the tub. Yes, I spoiled them, and they spoiled me.

Amsterdam was quaint with its canals and picturesque seventeenth-century houses. Going into the Anne Frank house, we walked behind the bookcase hiding a secret stairway up to the cramped rooms where the family hid. We could visualize this young girl writing down her experiences and dreams, then the cold realization that she would die at fifteen in a concentration camp.

In wonder, we walked down some of the streets famous for "window shopping," with prostitutes posing in picture windows. My wife, Anne, and I were there forty years later, finding the scene to still be a thriving attraction spotlighting the world's oldest profession.

While in Copenhagen, our Student Travel group stayed in a coed dorm at one of the universities. Danish college boys were soon happily visiting with my delighted girls.

The second day we were there, my group wanted to prepare American hamburgers for the local boys. In a grocery store at the meat counter, the butchers spoke no English. Ann pointed to what she believed to be hamburger meat. Putting a finger on each side of her head, she gave the international code for cows, "Moo, moo." The butcher laughed, nodding yes.

There were no American-style hamburger buns to be found anywhere. The girls were inventive as they improvised a Euro version of hamburgers. After serving everyone, like good Americans, we picked up the burgers with our hands and proceeded to eat.

The Danish boys did little to hide their surprise at what they deemed our gauche eating habits. They proceeded to demonstrate to us how Europeans properly dined: fork in left hand, cut the food with the knife, and place the now-filled fork in your mouth. The girls emphatically let them know that these were American burgers, eaten only by hand. Wanting to please, the boys immediately put down their utensils and followed suit.

For each country visited, Student Travel equipped the drivers with Michelin maps, the gold standard for European drivers. One old-timer advised me that Ike planned D-Day with Michelin maps. But I still made some wrong turns.

Crossing into Sweden, I have no idea where I erred. Neither would Ike. My guess is the girls wanted to see some of the Swedish countryside. We ended up on a dirt road neatly omitted from Mr. Michelin's map. We spied a lady walking with her son down the road ahead of us. She had a shopping basket in one hand and her son's hand in the other. The child was about eight years old. Of course, none of us knew a word of Swedish. I pointed at the road and raised my hands palms up, the universal sign of "I'm lost."

Our predicament was obvious. Mom spoke no English. After some hesitation, the child gave me directions to the main highway—in perfect English. We learned that in the Scandinavian countries, it was more economical to teach English in the early grades, obviating the need to translate textbooks into their native languages. The boy must have been a fast learner, much to our good fortune.

This experience brings me to the topic of young European men. Traveling around Europe, frequenting cafes and bars favored by our continental age group, the girls would be charmed by the young men they met. It was astounding how many of these fellows were counts, dukes, or some other equally impressive rank. Several times I lost one of my girls for a short while to a baron or count, even after the girls had figured out the pick-up line.

My lasting impression of European college men was imprinted on me in Heidelberg, Germany. This beautiful, quaint German town with its narrow streets and baroque houses was spared by the invading Americans in World War II. Its mayor sent an emissary to the US commander of the troops on the city's outskirts inviting him to inspect the city and confirm it had no military significance; the allied soldiers bypassed it, saving it for the enjoyment of Student Travel groups and thousands of others in the ensuing years after the war.

In Heidelberg, we frequented a German bierstube favored by students of the University of Heidelberg. Immediately we noticed dashing young men in white uniforms with red sashes across one shoulder draping to their waist. Atop their heads were red and white caps. What really made them stand out were the deep scars across their faces. On learning why they proudly sported the scars, the girls were impressed. So was I.

These were members of one of the five university "Korps," noted for their competitive beer drinking. More seriously, they dueled. Once a young man became a member of a Korp, he was obliged to fight at least one duel with a member of another Korp. Most chose to fight at least four or five. For the duels with pointed rapiers, they padded their chests and around their necks, and would wear thick, clear glasses over their eyes.

The only remaining vulnerable area was the face, where a gashing wound could be inflicted on tender skin. The duel would be fought until one of the combatants was cut on the cheek. Upon being wounded, many were known to tear open their wound and pour wine in it to enhance the scar when healed.

We learned that the duels were fought at the Hotel Die Hirschgasse, across the Neckar River from the university. Being curious, several of us Student Travel drivers crossed the river to the hotel's bierstube.

The owner brought our beers and beckoned us to another table. There, he proudly showed us Otto Von Bismarck's initials. The future chancellor of Germany had carved his initials there when he was a student in the 1830s. We asked about the dueling. With some cajoling, he led us to a high-ceilinged room with chairs circling the periphery.

Noting our confused looks, he pointed a finger up, then down. Raising and lowering our heads, we saw spattered blood, almost obliterating the ceiling and floor, silent witnesses to the hundreds of slashing rapiers.

Decades later, my wife, Anne, and I stayed at the Hirschgasse. I asked the owner to show us the dueling room. He noted that the hotel had been remodeled; dueling had been outlawed. Chuckling, he added, "You may be glad to know that where you're sleeping was once part of that room."

10

Europe Lessons Learned

UPON OUR ARRIVAL AT A CHARMING HOTEL in Paris, I had a surprise. Entering the lobby, the girls carrying their suitcases, I asked for our room keys. The concierge, wringing her hands and in some distress, informed me that the group occupying our rooms were still there. They were staying over because their bus needed repairs.

She assured me she had a nice hotel for my girls a few blocks away. Suspicions raised, I asked to see the other hotel before I would agree to a change of plans.

Leaving the girls in the lobby, she and I walked a few minutes and, *voila*! We were in the middle of the notorious Place Pigalle. Nearby was the famous Moulin Rouge nightclub, famed for its cancan dancers and the artist Toulouse-Lautrec. Pigalle was equally famous for its prostitutes, which I noted immediately.

She showed me the hotel. It was obvious this was not an inn for Texas coeds. It was used for hourly rather than nightly rates, as I noticed a hooker climbing the stairs ahead of us, customer in hand.

No, my girls were not staying there.

Returning to the hotel, I told the girls to leave their bags in the lobby and get comfortable. We were camping there until we got our rooms. Miraculously, our rooms appeared within thirty minutes.

I suspected the innkeeper negotiated a cheap rate at the bordello, wanting to pocket the difference of what Student Travel paid her and what our rooms could be rented for later that day. It was July, the height of the tourist season.

After that stir-up, it was my first night in Paris! The first sight on my list was the Eiffel Tower. Candy, a girl from another bus, and I grabbed my van. We were off to sightsee.

Having boasted she had two semesters of French, going by other cars, she was screaming "Eiffel Tower" in perfect English. The locals looked at us with amusement; "Crazy, stupid Americans," their faces seemed to say. Finally, I yelled, "Candy, ask in French!" She cried out, "I can't remember!" Then it dawned on her, "Le Tour E-fell," she yelled at the car next to us. Two hand signals from our new friends and two turns later, there it was. Breathtaking! Its lights brightly glittering on the River Seine, as the tourist-filled Bateaux Mouches boats passed beneath.

Two days later was the Fourth of July. We learned that in honor of our country's birthday, the grounds of the US embassy would welcome Americans in Paris, replete with hot dogs, fireworks, and flags. We mingled with other delighted Americans celebrating our country's birthday in the embassy's beautiful gardens, as cars rushed by on the nearby Place de la Concorde.

Being 1969, the only "freeways" in Europe were the autobahns in Germany and Austria and some autostradas in Italy. For the most part, all other major highways in European countries were two-lane. The "highway" from Paris to Bordeaux was a narrow two-lane roadway, flanked with trees on each side. Supposedly, the trees were first planted by Napolean to shade his marching troops.

Leaving Bordeaux, we crossed the Pyrenees into Basque country. It was overcast, chilly, and raining. The narrow, wet roads snaking over the mountains added to the mystery of this most ancient culture in Europe. My imagination wandered to World War II. It was over these mountains that Jewish and French refugees fled the Nazis, along with downed RAF and US airmen, desperately trying to escape to find friendly faces.

After crossing into Spain, we were reminded that this remained the country of the dictator Franco. Passing us on two speeding motorcycles were two members of the Civil Guard, with machine guns strapped to their backs. Having never seen weapons of this type, it gave us pause. But soon, we were in the streets of Pamplona. The Feast of San Fermin. The Running of the Bulls!

Sporting bota wine bags and mingling with other international students, we wandered over these old streets, happily partying and celebrating.

One exception stays with me many years later. In the early morning hours, I struck up a conversation with a French student. He was about my age. Friendly at first, he became belligerent, talking about "ugly Americans." I'm not sure what prompted his mood change, probably wine, but patriotism prompted mine. Looking at him, I sneered, "If it weren't for Americans, you'd be speaking German."

With that, he spat at the ground and walked off. As the morning sun hinted first light, it would soon be time for the bulls to run. And for young men to test their courage.

Making my way to the Calle de Santo Domingo, the narrow half-mile corridor enclosed by ancient walls, I found a vantage point to watch this spectacle. Both sides of the street were crowded, the spectators sitting on ancient walls, in this old quarter of Pamplona.

The crowd's cheers preceded the sight of young men, dressed in white, sporting red bandanas and running, the bulls close behind. A few fellows stumbled, and the bulls usually jumped over them. If a bull lowered its head, he usually shoved rather than gored the men on the ground. These daredevils walked away with mostly bruises to show for their courage.

From my perch, the excitement was over in less than ninety seconds as the men and bulls rushed by. With that excitement over, we made our way for the afternoon corrida at the Plaza de Toros.

The angry and confused bull entered the arena, having spent his entire life in a pasture, seldom seeing a man afoot. Now in this unfamiliar ring, he was surrounded by hundreds of yelling people. Running around the perimeter, he hooked his sharp horns at the barriers that protected the *"cuadrilla,"* the matador and his toreros. They soon entered the arena, taunting the bull with their large yellow and pink capes. The sharp banderilleros and picadors pierced the bull's shoulders. Now the bull's head sagged for the matador's final killing thrust.

The matador then strides in alone, dressed in gold or silver. He is an athlete, with agility, grace, and poise. Alone, he faces the bull. His defense is his courage and a small red cape, with his *estocada*, a small sword first used to spread the cape outward and then to aim for the kill.

With a series of passes, the bull comes within inches of his body as the matador performs to the adoration of hundreds of *"Oles!"*

Following this ballet, the matador taunts the bull with his cape one final time. Standing on his toes, as the bull rushes forward, the matador holds the sword aloft and thrusts downward, the horns coming within inches of his body. The sword pierces the bull's heart and lungs. The bull falls—*muerto*. The crowd is screaming in adulation. The matador circles the arena, flowers landing at his feet. And he pauses before a beautiful senorita, handing a rose up to her.

Leaving Pamplona the next day for Barcelona on another two-lane road, we spied a wagon on a hilltop. Two of the girls yelled, "Gypsies!"

I pulled up. It was a gypsy wagon adorned with carved decorations. A gaunt horse was standing nearby as a couple and two children rose from their cooking fire.

The girls grabbed their cameras. The man and the children immediately held out their hands. We scrambled for some pesetas and handed them out the window.

Placated for only a moment, the man looked at the money. Deeming it insufficient, he and the children grabbed rocks and hurled them at the bus. I jammed the van in reverse and sped off the hill as fast as a VW bus can speed. But we were safe on our way to Barcelona.

A challenge for European drivers was the passage to Berlin through East Germany, about a three-hour trip on one of Hitler's original autobahns, paved in the original brick. These autobahns gave Ike the idea that would become the United States Interstate Highway System.

Any vehicle entering or leaving East Germany was subject to a search. Luggage was pulled and inspected. A mirror on wheels was passed beneath the vehicle. This procedure was a half-hour ordeal, the soldiers displaying a serious demeanor.

The second time I drove across East Germany, the route was the same, but the soldiers' demeanors would be quite different. One of the Student Travel drivers had had a death in the family, and he returned to Texas. Having put my girls on a plane at the Brussels airport for their return to Texas, I learned the other girls and their bus were stranded in Vienna. Skip Smith, the Student Travel coordinator, told me to hop the next train to Vienna. I would be the girls' new driver.

These girls were Tri-Delts. The criteria to pledge Delta Delta Delta at Texas were twofold: You had to be blonde and gorgeous. After picking them up and taking charge of their bus, we were off to Berlin.

It dawned on me that the East German soldiers were young and loaded with testosterone. Inside my van were six beautiful Texas coeds. I explained the international sensitivity of this situation to the girls. They got the picture.

Before the checkpoint, we stopped on the west side for candy and other goodies. Being 1969 and smokers, we pulled out US cigarettes to give to the soldiers with the other treats.

The girls piled out of the van with a couple of strategic buttons undone, handing out their gifts, hugging the soldiers, and planting kisses on their cheeks. At this point, inspecting our van was the furthest thing from the minds of these East German boys. They, with blushing red faces, were inspecting the girls.

After a minute of this lovefest, an old sergeant emerged from his hut. Sizing up the situation, he pointed a finger at me, the girls, the bus, and the autobahn. I understood. Without a word exchanged, I got the girls back in the bus, abandoning their new, disappointed friends. The border inspection by the notorious East German soldiers lasted less than two minutes.

Other adventures:

- Staying in the palatial estate of Count Gustav Ottolenghi in the Italian hills of Liguria. The private chapel's entry doors were from the Vatican, as the Count had donated new doors to the church. At lunch, we enjoyed his wine as we looked down on his vineyard below us. Then on to the charming port town of Portofino.

- Experiencing the horrors of the Dachau concentration camp, where thousands of Jews and other "undesirables" were cruelly abused and executed, I was depressed, along with the girls, some in tears.

- Trying to get a beer in Amsterdam. We had been in Germany and picked up phrases like *"Ein grossen bier, bitte"*—a large beer, please. When I said this, the old innkeeper in Amsterdam refused to serve us. When I inquired in English, he explained, "I thought you were goddamned Germans. They invaded us twice and will do it again." After that, he was very friendly.

- Going through Checkpoint Charlie, from the American sector in Berlin, crossing the infamous wall into East Berlin. World War II had ended just over twenty-five years before, but in East Berlin, many buildings appeared just as they had after the Russians invaded in April 1945.

- Walking into the casino at Monte Carlo with its stunning red carpet, gold curtains, and chandeliers.

- Walking through snow in July in Zermatt, Switzerland, at the base of the Matterhorn.

- Staying in a guest house outside Salzburg, Austria, strolling in the night and finding the church where the wedding scene in the Sound of Music was filmed.

That summer in Europe, thanks to Oliver and Student Travel, prepared me for numerous trips Anne and I would take there over the years.

11

Number 365

IF YOU WERE A MALE AND IN college in the late '60s, the Vietnam War was the overriding event that pervaded your life. The conflict became severe in 1964 with the Gulf of Tonkin incident, where US warships clashed with North Vietnamese ships. Four years later was the bloodiest year of the war. More than 58,000 American servicemen would die in that futile cause, many of them drafted.

If you did not go to Vietnam, you knew someone who did. My high school friend Dennis Olson went to UT on a Navy scholarship. Because of his high grades, he could elect to become a Marine in his junior year.

Lieutenant Olson spent two tours of duty in 'Nam. When he returned to Texas, he told me that at night in the jungle, he would look at his legs, wondering if they would be there the next day.

When I met my UT roommate, Gip Brown, he was already a Vietnam veteran. He returned as an ardent anti-war advocate. Having always been a political and news junkie—and with a bit of self-interest—I was very much against the war and joined in the protests that permeated UT and other campuses nationwide.

The military "recruited" many of its soldiers through the draft. The Selective Service Act required every young man who reached the age of eighteen to register with his local draft board. There were exceptions to being drafted, such as student deferments, conscientious objectors, and ministers. I was never clear on how the local draft boards picked the draftees, but I did understand what a lottery was.

On December 1, 1969, a new selection method was employed. Blue tabs with dates representing all 366 days of the year, including February 29, were randomly selected. The first date to be pulled was September 14. If that was your birthday, you would certainly be called up. The further down the list your birthdate was drawn, the less likely the odds you would be drafted.

All the Phi Psi men were glued to the house television on the late autumn evening of the drawing. As the dates were called, there were some sighs and groans. After approximately fifty dates were pulled, my birth date had not appeared.

I had to leave for my evening shift at KNOW. When I got in the car, I had missed several dates being called. Listening to the radio intently, I made the short five-minute drive to the station. My newsman was continuing to read the numbers on the air as I rushed into the newsroom. I looked over his shoulder as he read from the AP wire machine. I tried to scan the former pages without interfering with his line of sight, without success at seeing any missed numbers.

I contented myself with reading the incoming teletype. We were now in the 300s, then there it was, number 365, February 26: my birthday. While feeling sorry for the guys who were on the early picks, that was the only drawing I ever won. It was a big one. There was no way that I would be drafted.

I had planned to attend law school since I was a young boy, but KNOW and major market radio exposure made my thoughts wander. Radio was fun and exciting. I was on the ground floor of a promising career. I could envision sales, management, and owning my own stations. When I mentioned this to Dad, he said, "Go to law school. Radio will still be there in three years." The message sank in.

When it was time to leave for law school in Houston, I went into the program director's office and told him my plans. He looked at me, remarking, "Why do you want to do that? You have a great future in broadcasting." Though I dared not say it to him, the response that immediately came to my mind was, "I don't want to be a forty-year-old teeny-bopper disc jockey."

When I began the application process for law school, I assumed I would go to UT. Most people who went to UT then had no desire to leave Austin. I was one of them. Each law school had different admission requirements, but one thing they had in common was a minimum score, a combination of your undergraduate grade point average and the Law School Admissions Test score.

At UT Law, the minimum score for admission was 1100. The school informed me that I had scored 1085, fifteen points shy.

I made an appointment with the dean of admissions to see if I could do anything to remedy this situation. Dean Thomas Jefferson Gibson was a courtly man. He sincerely seemed to want to help me. He explained that my 2.6 UT GPA was the problem.

I had spent some time at Texas Tech and had a 3.5 GPA from that time. Wouldn't that put me over the top? Yes, it would, but Texas would not accept the Tech grades. After all, Texas was *The University.*

Dean Gibson proceeded to tell me that I could get into any other law school in the state and asked, "Do you intend to practice law in Texas?" After telling him that was my plan, without hesitation, he said, "Go to the University of Houston."

I took his advice. I was off to the Bayou City.

12

Highs and Lows in Law School

PROFESSOR JAMES HIPPARD STRODE INTO MY FIRST class on my first day of UH law school: Criminal Procedure. The law school professor quickly imparted, "The most important thing I can teach you about criminal law, and remember this, 'You may beat the rap, but you can't beat the ride downtown.'" He was telling us that if you try to argue with a cop, they can still take you to jail. You may get out, but you will probably get in the back seat of a police car first.

Before Professor Hippard's class, I had already learned some things about law school, the first being there is an adage describing each of the three years of law school. The first year they scare you to death, the second year they work you to death, and the third year they bore you to death. It was true for me.

My first-year class's introduction to law school was a meeting with some third-year students the week before courses began. They told us that unlike every other course we had taken from grade school through college, there would be no pop quizzes, midterm exams, or papers to be graded during the semester. Your grade for the semester would be based on one test: the final exam. As if that was not enough to cause some concern, the next line was, "Look to your left, look to your right. One of you won't be here next year."

Oh, how comforting.

We were told that our textbooks would contain only appellate cases, decisions that we would read and analyze and then recite in class. Once in class, we had the joy of not knowing when or whom the professor would call on to recite a case, give its facts, give the decision, and explain the legal reasoning behind it. The professor would then interrogate the student to elicit mistakes and oversights in their recitation. This teaching method is called the Socratic Method, based on Socrates teaching students through instructive arguments and dialogue. It had another teaching purpose: The professor's questions resembled cross-examination.

My most memorable experience with this form of education happened in my first semester in Contracts I. Professor Eliezer Ereli had been an original Israeli freedom fighter. His thick accent and salt and pepper hair constantly fell over his left eyebrow. He was no-nonsense.

He would strut around the class in a cocksure manner, peering over his half-rim glasses at his roster of students. That was when the next poor soul would be selected to recite one of the cases assigned for that day. The professor was unforgiving in his critical questions. Many times after finishing their recitation, the student would wonder if they had read the wrong case.

The Case of Rosie the Cow was a staple of first-year contract law. The cow's seller and buyer struck a deal with the belief that Rosie was barren. Before she was delivered to the buyer, the seller discovered Rosie was pregnant. Rosie was now much more valuable than the agreed-upon price since she was able to produce little Rosies and Ferdinands. The seller refused to relinquish her to the buyer. The case ended up on appeal. The higher court ruled the contract void under the theory of mutual mistake. They thought Rosie couldn't have babies—but she could.

I always tried to be very prepared for Professor Ereli. The fall day when we studied Rosie was no different. I had read, outlined, and studied her case from nose to tail. When he called me to recite, I was ready. My discourse lasted about five minutes. I knew I had nailed the case.

Professor Ereli looked at me over his glasses. Calmly, in his thick accent, he slowly said, "Mr. Conner, your problem is you think like a student, not like a lawyer."

He then proceeded, as Socrates would have it, to ask me questions, illustrating how little I understood about Rosie.

When it came time for final exams, I left the contracts classroom deflated. I knew I had failed. When the grades were posted some weeks later, mine was an 83, the second-highest grade in the class.

Jerry Mabry was a close high school friend from Lamesa who graduated from TCU and enrolled with me in law school. It was good to have a friend to commiserate with in what I knew would be a challenging year. We rented an apartment in the Stella Link area of Houston at the beginning of our first semester.

A typical week for us in that semester: Sunday, start studying for Monday, get up the next morning, go to classes, study between classes, return to the apartment, eat dinner, and study until the 10 p.m. news. Repeat until Friday afternoon. That's when Jerry and I would go to the Sage Discount Store on the corner of Beechnut and Loop 610 and buy a case of Shiner beer for $4.99. Between Friday night and Sunday at noon, we would consume the beer, catch up on sleep, and then start the routine over again.

By the time fall grades were posted a few weeks into the spring semester, we had a handle on law school. We quit the manic routine that was our introduction to graduate studies and began to lead a more normal life. Yes, we continued to study hard, but we found a groove: a few hours of study per day until it was time to cram for exams using our well-kept class notes.

As my class progressed through law school, we were puzzled about the relationship of our courses to the larger world of being an attorney. What do contracts have to do with torts? What does court procedure have to do with wills and estates? What does commercial law have to do with constitutional law?

There is no way to explain our epiphany during our third year, but eventually we just got it. Contracts could involve a tort. The court procedure was needed to try a tort case, will contest, commercial case, or myriad other things. Whatever area of law was practiced, there must be an understanding of all areas of the law.

Yes, Professor Ereli, I began to think like a lawyer.

13

Anne

BOB MACINTYRE AND I MET AS FIRST-YEAR law students. We had classes together and struck up a great friendship that lasts to this day.

Bob's dad was a greatly respected doctor, the head of radiology at Methodist Hospital. Bob grew up in Houston, and his was a well-known family. Bob introduced me to many friends he'd grown up with in Houston. Many became my friends as well.

I was fortunate enough to become a part of his family. The MacIntyres liked to entertain in an environment that included their children. Many nights in law school, I was at their house with Bob and his siblings for the cocktail hour or dinner.

For the most part, the girls I dated in law school were not the type to bring home to mom.

In September 1973, we had finished law school and were awaiting the bar exam results. Bob Susman, a law school classmate, was celebrating his birthday. His grandfather was one of Houston's elite merchants who founded Battelstein's Department Store on the edge of River Oaks. Having grown up in that atmosphere in Houston, Susman knew a wide variety of people. Neither MacIntyre nor I had dates, so we went to the party stag.

As we left the party, MacIntyre remarked, "Conner, if you're going to make it in Houston, you need to start dating some nicer girls."

My response: "Like who?"

Bob said, "You met Anne Garwood tonight."

I vaguely remembered meeting Anne. I did recall that she was beautiful. I thought her husband had accompanied her and that they were not getting along. I later learned he was just a date, and she was miserable with the guy.

Anne was a secretary in the trust department at Southern National Bank on Main Street, founded by some of Anne's father's friends. In its early days, it was known as the "Martini" Bank. Anne will be the first to admit she was not a great secretary, but with her godfather on the board of directors, her skills were not that important.

The law office where I was clerking was two blocks away. I called Anne and asked her to have dinner. She said no, but we could meet for a drink. It would have to be early. "I'm going to the opera with my mother," Anne told me. My West Texas brain computed that as a brush-off, so I called MacIntyre.

"Conner, I promise you that's the truth," said Bob, the matchmaker.

Anne and I met for drinks. Two nights later, we had our second date. Within a few days, we were together constantly.

Anne was stunning. She had no fear. Having grown up in Houston, she had a wide circle of friends she saw regularly. We were having the best times of our young lives: dinner out many nights, introductions to her many friends and family, sailing in Galveston, Broadway shows, and, yes, even the opera.

To say our romance was a whirlwind is an understatement. It took less than three weeks before I popped the question. She said yes! The first person we told was Bob MacIntyre.

Anne then proceeded to educate a West Texas boy about real life in the big city. She took this young man who had always dressed in shiny suits, loafers, and boots to Brooks Brothers. I learned to dress in conservative wool suits, white button-down shirts, traditional ties, and cap-toed laced shoes.

We were invited to parties at the Houston and River Oaks country clubs. Some of Anne's family gave us a party at the Bayou Club, the most exclusive club in Houston. She introduced me to a new life and many people. I absorbed as much as I could, learning details of social life in a big city.

We married in the chapel of St. John the Divine Episcopal Church in Houston. It was a gorgeous February day. Following the afternoon wedding, the reception was at the Junior League. Afterward, some friends took us to the airport to board our honeymoon plane to Paris.

My feeling was the most romantic honeymoon possible was a trip to Paris. During the all-night flight on Air France, the cabin attendants were most attentive, knowing we were honeymooners. On arriving in the City of Light, I could barely contain my excitement.

We stayed in the Hotel Ambassador. Its most famous guest was Charles Lindbergh, who stayed there in 1927, after his historic solo flight to Paris.

We did all the usual sightseeing, frequenting the storied museums and brasseries. One night, in a small café, we were seated next to an older French couple. The bereted Frenchman spoke excellent English. Being a World War II buff, I asked him if he was in France during the war. That began one of the most fascinating evenings of our lives.

He was a resistance fighter during the war, risking his life, avoiding capture by the Nazis, which would have meant sure torture and death. He didn't have to tell me that. The previous afternoon, we'd visited the Liberation Museum of Paris, where the displays graphically showcased the risks, torture, deaths, and accomplishments of the resistance fighters. We left the café and proceeded in a cab, with our new friend providing a history lesson from the front seat.

This amazing war veteran guided the driver through the wet streets of Paris, pointing out locations of his encounters with the Nazis that took place as the allies closed in. "We were behind a barricade here," he pointed at a bridge over the Seine. "We knew the Americans were coming and so did the Nazis. They attacked us. My best friend was next to me. He was shot and killed."

As the evening came to an end, the taxi pulled up to a bistro. I insisted that our new friends join us for a brandy. The evening concluded and, over my objection, he insisted that he buy the drinks. "We owe a lot to Americans," he said.

As I write this some fifty years later, one thing is sure: Anne deserves mountains of credit for whatever success I have enjoyed. She took my rough edges off and taught me to be comfortable with people of great wealth and position. She introduced me to people from her parents' generation and persons she grew up with, many of whom became clients.

My law practice grew. Anne was a successful real estate agent/broker. We were able to enjoy a life with two great children: Emily was born in 1977, joined by Will in 1980.

Although we have had ups and downs and everything in between, we have always had each other. We still do.

14

The Bookie Murder

IT WAS A BEAUTIFUL SPRING MORNING IN Houston. Lying in bed, I was reading the paper, the TV morning news playing in in the background. Anne suddenly turned to me, "Did you hear that? There was a murder in River Oaks last night."

A murder in Houston's premiere neighborhood, home to executives, doctors, and lawyers, was unheard of. The wealthy denizens typically settled their differences with lawyers, not guns.

When I walked into the office, my office manager, Barbara Bland, said, "Did you hear the news? Doris Angleton was murdered."

An attractive, willowy woman with flawless skin and auburn hair had walked into my office five months earlier. It was no surprise that a River Oaks image consultant regularly hired her "ideal body type" for local fashion seminars. This lady wanted a divorce. Her name was Doris Angleton.

When she came to my office the first time, she told me that she and her husband Robert had twin daughters aged twelve and proceeded to give me basic information about her family and marriage.

"So, what does Bob do for a living?" I asked. She told me her husband owned interests in a courier service, a shopping center, a golf course, and a tennis club.

She calmly added, "And he is the biggest bookmaker in Houston."

I was accustomed to hearing unusual tales from clients, but this was a first. I successfully held my surprise in check. Doris handed me two ledger sheets. The far-left column held sequential numbers representing the hidden identities of the bettors. The following seven columns were the days of the week. Below those days were black and red numbers. To the far right were notations in Bob's handwriting. Though it made no sense to me, it was enlightening. So this was how Houston's most successful bookie kept his records.

Both Doris and Bob had previously been married to other people. Bob was infatuated with Doris from the first time he saw her, telling her then-husband, "If you ever want to get rid of that pretty lady, let me know about it."

Bob had a brusque personality, with little sense of humor and no time for small talk. His laser interest was making money. Consequently, he did not fit in with the crowd he longed to be a part of—the wealthy up-and-coming Houston baby boomers. But he did see them as potential clients. Doris was attractive and socially savvy, with an outgoing personality and looks to match. Bob wanted to be a part of her scene.

Bob successfully used Doris. They bought a house in River Oaks and joined the Briar Club, a tennis and swimming spot favored by young professionals and people of wealth. Bob was getting new clients who had money to spare.

He would blatantly take bets while he was at the Briar Club, keeping a pager and cell phone in plain sight, checking it often. His behavior was evident to many members of the club. At one point, there was a discussion among some board members about removing the Angleton family as members. It never happened. The belief was that the club did not want to embarrass Doris or the girls.

It was a poorly kept secret among many River Oaks residents that Bob was an outlaw, an illegal bookmaker, charging a ten percent fee for his services. His wealthy clientele included one man "whose family's name was on buildings and streets all over town."

Bob furnished rent-free apartments to "associates" who took many of the bets and, along with Bob, promptly delivered any winnings. The police estimated that between twenty and forty million dollars passed through Bob's book each year. With his ten percent commission, he was taking home millions himself.

When Doris came to see me, the marriage had fallen apart, at least as far as she was concerned. After fourteen years of marriage, Bob treated Doris like a possession rather than a wife. She felt no emotion was left between them. She had also connected with a soulmate on the internet, prompting an affair. She was ready to escape from Bob.

Doris told me her main concerns: How to keep Bob from making off with the cash and how she could clear up any potential criminal problems she might face. After all, she did enjoy the illegal money that was not reported to the IRS. Fortunately, Doris knew there were safe deposit boxes in banks where a lot of cash was stashed.

In solving her first concern, protecting the cash, I advised her that we should name the banks in the divorce action where she suspected cash was being kept. This was necessary to prevent them from opening the boxes for Bob or anyone else. Not wanting the banks to think we were after them in any sense, and coining a new term, they would be sued as "nominal respondents." The petition would state that they were named in the litigation solely to protect the boxes.

Regarding her second concern, I told her we would hire a tax attorney to investigate her best course of action at the appropriate time.

When a divorce is filed, it is customary to immediately have one of the parties removed from the residence, usually the husband. Doris's plans were different. She and Bob were peacefully coexisting. She wanted to stay in the house with their twelve-year-old daughters for a few months so the girls would be further along in the school year. Her instructions to me: "Get everything ready to go. I will tell you when."

She instructed me not to call her house or cell phone in order to keep Bob in the dark. If I needed to talk to her, I would call a friend she named, who would message her.

In early February 1997, she was ready. I filed her divorce petition. Doris signed an affidavit supporting our request to enjoin the banks, reading, "My husband deals in substantial amounts of cash that is held in safe deposit boxes. Only he has the keys. I fear he will go to the banks and take the money. I will have no way to prove the existence of the cash."

The judge signed my order granting the injunctions.

On a Monday at 9 a.m., my process servers delivered the orders to the banks simultaneously. One hour later, Bob was served with the same injunction and a longer list of orders directed solely at Doris and him. These were standard divorce orders mutually enjoining both parties from hiding assets, harming one another, hiding the children, and the like. In other words, keep the status quo.

At the time we filed, Doris sent Bob a letter: "I retained a lawyer in December when things seemed so volatile and I didn't know what you were going to do next. The undercurrent of volatility is still there, and it is frightening. I have followed the attorney's advice. He's enjoining the bank boxes if there are any, as I don't know what steps you have already taken."

She explained that she was frightened about what he might do and asked him to stay calm, help with the girls, and try to move on to the next step. Bob's initial reaction was to shower her with gifts and attention, professing his love and desire to work things out. It did not work.

Bob hired Bill de la Garza as his attorney. Bill was a friend of mine and a good lawyer. I took that as a positive sign, as Bill and I always collegially worked together. Neither of us subscribed to the Rambo tactics some lawyers, such as Joe Jamail, engaged in.

Before we had the final draft of the agreed upon temporary injunctions, de la Garza called. Would Doris agree to lift the bank injunctions if both she and Bob were present to open the boxes together? Calling Doris, she agreed. They would go to the banks and split the money in the safety deposit boxes.

On a February day, they went to Northern Trust Company, where three boxes were located, and removed $3.2 million: two piles, one for Doris and one for Bob, $1.6 million each.

This division of cash was advantageous for both. Bob had no desire to explain to a judge that he opposed the bank injunction. The boxes did hold illegal gambling money. He likely needed the cash for operating expenses because he still had bets to pay out. With Doris's $1.6 million, she did not have to worry about Bob holding the purse strings while the divorce went forward.

De la Garza and I also agreed on a date to file sworn inventories. A sworn inventory in a divorce is nothing more than a balance sheet. Each party asserts what they believe is the community and separate property, the values of such assets, and debts. It is the starting point for a lawyer to decide the documents needed from the other party and to determine other entities that might be subpoenaed. I would ask Bob to produce, among other things, all safety deposit box records, copies of all his bookie ledger sheets, his computer hard drives, a list of all his bettors, and financial statements from all his legitimate business interests. These requests would go back for five years.

I had forensic computer experts available to examine Bob's computer and download all financial information that might be needed. Such examination might also show who his bettors were.

I believed that Bob would provide me with his computer, only I anticipated that he would clean any information that might be damaging to him. When a computer is "cleaned," a computer expert can determine the amount of deleted data and the date it happened—providing proof that Bob had tampered with evidence. While it might deny me wanted information, it would subject him to sanctions and give the judge a good reason to make an unequal estate division that heavily favored Doris.

In addition, I had accountants available to examine all the records of his legitimate businesses, do on-site inspections, interview the managers, and render expert opinions as to the value of Bob's interests. A real estate appraiser would be hired to provide an expert opinion on the value of the real property.

Once we gathered all the documents, I would have the opportunity to put Bob under oath and take his deposition: Who are your bookie associates, what is your history in the business, and what have you used your cash for? My experts would also provide me with questions for information they might need to do their reports.

I believed we would never get to that point. I knew he would have no desire to be deposed under oath. I also knew that Doris would be satisfied with a sizeable cash payment, and Bob would want to buy his peace. Anticipating he would also give her a large amount of cash, the house, significant child support payments, and private school tuition, including college, I felt certain we would reach an agreement.

While preparing our document requests and arranging for expert witnesses, Doris reported that things were okay, but she had one question that weighed heavily on her. She and I both were confident there was more cash. She knew that she would be a millionaire. Just one problem: What if the IRS came along? There would be taxes, penalties, interest, and a strong possibility of criminal charges. She did not want that cloud hanging over her head.

Not being a tax lawyer, I referred her to Eddie Urquhart, a tax attorney who had previously worked for the IRS. I said, "Doris, I think this is what he will tell you. You and Bob must go back, amend your returns, pay the tax, penalty, and interest, and come clean." That would relieve any possibility of criminal charges against her. Eddie's advice during their visit was identical to mine.

While Bob was coaching their daughters' softball game six days later, someone entered their residence. That someone put seven bullets in Doris's head and five in her chest, wanting to make sure she was very dead. When I heard she was murdered, I immediately thought that she told Bob about Eddie's advice, and Bob had her murdered.

The morning after her death, reporters were at the courthouse looking for any filings concerning Bob. They quickly found the divorce filing, and my phone started ringing. They all wanted to know if I thought Bob had her killed, if he was abusive, and if he threatened her. I was not going to touch any of that.

Before her death, Doris and I were confident Bob had other safety deposit boxes stuffed with cash. I believed that we would find them as the divorce continued, and later, the police did—to the tune of $7 million.

Bob had plenty of motivation for Doris to disappear. He faced giving up more than half of everything he had; if they were going to file amended returns, it would cost him a fortune. Failing to file the returns, he could be looking at penitentiary time for tax evasion. Doris wanted to go straight, not Bob.

Doris's funeral was at St. Luke's United Methodist Church, one of the largest worship houses in Houston, located on the edge of River Oaks. It was packed with four hundred mourners.

On April 27, 1997, ten days after the murder, my firm offered a $5,000 reward for the arrest and conviction of anyone responsible for the heinous murder of Doris Angleton. She had been referred to me by a friend of mine who happened to be a Howard Hughes heir, who contributed an additional $20,000. Another $25,000 came in from Bob Angleton. The total: $50,000.

Naturally, the police suspected Bob. The first thing he told them was a surprise. "Yes, I am a bookie. I also work for the Houston Police Department." Unbeknownst to the arresting officers, Bob was an informant. His contact was a Detective Fielder. Bob would turn in his competitors, who would get arrested, then Bob would take over their clients. Fielder later retired and became a bookmaker himself. Bob ratted him out, and he was arrested. And then the detectives learned about Bob's brother, Roger, who was six years Bob's senior.

Roger was a loser. He lived off and on in California, Texas, and Nevada. At one time, Bob hired him as a bookie associate, but Roger did not have the mathematical mind to succeed, so Bob fired him.

Roger sent Bob a letter asking for $200,000, saying he had documents to prove Bob's illegal activities. The money was for Roger's silence. Pay up, or "I will make you pay dearly. I will hurt you in a way that will be with you the rest of your life." Bob gave the police the letter. It was dated six weeks before Doris's murder.

The police were now trying to find Roger without much luck. They learned there was a warrant out for his arrest in San Diego for theft of prescription drugs. And the Houston detectives let the San Diego police know that Roger was wanted for questioning in Houston.

Roger was arrested in Las Vegas in July 1997. The San Diego police were notified and advised the Houston detectives, who then headed to Las Vegas.

When Roger was arrested, the police found a briefcase in his room. There was over $64,000 in cash and several paper money wrappers. One had Bob's fingerprints. They also found typewritten notes with the gate and alarm codes for the Angleton house and a cassette tape recording.

On the tape, two men were discussing alarm codes, and how a woman, who one man called "Doris," typically entered the house. "The first gunshot has to be on the money." Both Roger and Bob were arrested.

Roger Angleton was never tried for the murder of Doris. He committed suicide in the Harris County jail on February 17, 1998. He inflicted fifty cuts on himself with a razor blade and left a note where he took full credit for the murder, absolving Bob. This note would not come into evidence at Bob's murder-for-hire trial. The court ruled it was hearsay.

Bob was charged with murder for hire in state district court. The tape recording was admitted. Witnesses disputed whether it was Bob's voice. I anticipated the twin daughters, now sixteen, would testify.

When I finished my own testimony, I walked by the prosecutor, Lynn McClellan. I said, "Lynn, those two girls will say, 'That's not my Daddy's voice.' When they do, that jury will not make them orphans."

That is precisely what happened. The jury found Bob not guilty.

But Bob was not free from the legal system. The United States Attorney came after him.

On March 1, 2001, I was sitting in the witness box in a federal courtroom, having been subpoenaed by a grand jury considering the indictment of Robert Angleton for the offense of murder for hire, gambling, and money laundering. I had been a lawyer for twenty-seven years. This was a new experience.

A grand jury decides whether to return an indictment, also known as a formal criminal charge against a person. Prosecutors bring in witnesses so they and the grand jurors can ask questions, always in a closed hearing. No one except witnesses, prosecutors, and grand jury members are allowed in the room. The potential defendant and his lawyers are not among them.

During my turn on the witness stand, the prosecutor stated, "You are a witness, you are not a target, you are not a suspect, you are not a subject of any of those things."

Well, I knew that. This speech was standard procedure to relieve a witness of any potential concerns about criminal charges. I knew I was *not* any of those things, but it was nice to hear it out loud.

As though echoing the questions I had answered three years before in Bob's state murder trial, I went through the details of my meetings with Doris, filing the divorce, our game plan, how they paid for the house (in cash), and Doris's consultation with a tax lawyer.

Early in my testimony, the assistant US attorney asked, "Do you think he had some involvement in her murder?"

My response: "Do you want me to speculate?"

This question surprised me. In a formal trial, witnesses cannot be asked to speculate—to guess what the facts may be. A witness must have personal knowledge to testify. I gave a lengthy response that said, yes, I thought he was involved.

Then I made my thoughts clear: "I don't know that this man did anything wrong. You are asking me to speculate. And there are a lot of things that go into why I would think that. Maybe we watch too much TV and movies, and maybe we've read too many books.

"The only other alternative would be somebody was there to hijack her and follow her into her driveway. We've heard of these types of crimes. They see your Rolex as you shop in a drugstore and follow you home. But it seems a stretch for a hijacker to have done everything that was done to her, and the evidence indicates that the murderer was already in the house." I stated the obvious, "It leads me to believe this was a setup."

Since I could not remain in the grand jury room, I don't know what other evidence the jurors heard. Whatever it was, it was enough. The US grand jury indicted Bob for all the charges the United States attorney requested.

The trial was set to begin. The prosecutors asked me to come to their offices in the federal courthouse to prepare me as a witness.

That summer day in 2002 I walked into a large room in the federal courthouse in Houston. The walls were covered in exhibits, witness outlines, and case research. There were two lawyers, two paralegals, and secretarial staff. I spent two hours with them going over my testimony and what they would question me about. I was amazed at the amount of preparation they had done. I learned things about the Angleton case that I had never heard before. I was reminded of things I had forgotten. This experience taught me one thing: No one should want the power of the United States Department of Justice coming after them.

Our time that day was wasted. A few days before trial, Bob boarded a plane for Amsterdam with $135,000 in cash inside a checked bag and a carry-on. At the Houston airport, a ticket agent told Bob there was something sticky on his passport. Bob knew that it was from the cheap glue he'd used to put it together. To his surprise, the agent checked him through. Upon landing in the Netherlands, his luck ran out. His fake passport didn't fool the Dutch customs agent.

Because of international treaties and European law, the Dutch court would not order Bob's extradition back to the States as long as he faced the death penalty. The federal prosecutors agreed to drop the murder charge but would go forward on new passport and tax fraud charges. In September 2004, one year after his international arrest, Bob was brought back to the United States. He pleaded guilty to passport and tax fraud and was sentenced to twelve years in federal prison. He was released in 2014.

The Angleton case brought me a great deal of publicity. *48 Hours* came to my office. Local television reporters had interviewed me in the past, but their preparation was no comparison to CBS News. A crew arrived at my office at 8 a.m. They had the building shut the air conditioning off so there would be no ambient sound. They set up lighting and arranged chairs. The crew did sound checks and had everything ready when Richard Schlesinger, the reporter, arrived.

The crew also placed a fan at Schlesinger's feet, pointing upward, so he could stay cool, even if the rest of us had to go without AC. The interview lasted about thirty minutes. About halfway through, I moved the fan toward me with my foot. I was now the beneficiary of cooler air.

The interview concluded and Schlesinger left. The crew was laughing and congratulating me for that small act of defiance. They thought Schlesinger was "an arrogant asshole."

To this day, Bob and his daughters contend that he is innocent of Doris's murder.

In a bit of irony, while Bob was awaiting his trials in Houston, he lived around the corner from me.

15

The Blue Law Cases

THE TEXAS BLUE LAW WAS A CONFUSING list of forty-two items that could not be sold on consecutive Saturdays and Sundays. The law forced many stores to close on Sundays (or Saturdays). Its name came from the original 1863 Sunday closing statute bound in blue paper.

The banned items included clothing, shoes, furniture, kitchenware, china, home appliances, and a myriad of other items. If you went into a grocery store on Sunday, you would find some sections cordoned off—all of it merchandise that fell under the Blue Law. Other stores, like those selling hardware, were forced to close. The district and county attorneys could sue to enforce this law, but by 1984, it was so unpopular that elected officials had no desire to enforce it.

But citizens and private entities were also allowed to enforce it. In 1984, Bob MacIntyre was hired by the Retail Merchants Association of Houston to enforce the Texas Blue Law. He asked me to be his cocounsel. I gladly agreed. Our client, the Retail Merchants Association, consisted of large department stores like

Joske's, Saks Fifth Avenue, Neiman Marcus, and Foley's, the largest retailers in the city at that time.

Many mom-and-pop stores and some big box stores like Academy Sporting Goods and Handy Dan were violating the law. The RMA wanted to force these stores to close on Sundays. Those staying open on Sundays had a competitive advantage over our client's stores. These high-end retailers had no desire to open Sundays, primarily because it hurt their bottom line.

Maury Aresty was the association's executive director, a veteran retailer and former head of Donaldson's, Minneapolis's most prominent department store. On Sundays, he would select stores in violation, visit them, and purchase a prohibited item. Of course, he made sure he saved the item and the dated receipt. His actions gave us the only evidence we needed to file a successful suit for enforcement: a witness who could prove the store was open on Sunday and that it sold a prohibited item.

Every Monday morning, Maury would provide us with a list of the stores he'd visited. We would file our lawsuits, asking for an order prohibiting the stores from opening on Sundays, thus closing them on Sunday.

The law and the appellate cases were straightforward. The stores would argue that the law was vague and selective and that the Retail Merchants Association was discriminating as to their targets. The only problem these stores had was the law, which was clear. And there were numerous appellate cases upholding it. We started a winning streak.

At first, the stores we were suing were mom-and-pop operations. I vividly recall that one of the stores specialized in socks: Sock It to Me, and we did. After several wins, the smaller stores got the message. They did not want to be the next target of the RMA. But our clients set their sights on the larger big box stores.

Academy Sports and Outdoors started as an army surplus store in San Antonio in the 1930s. Now with large stores throughout Texas, they sold everything related to sports and the outdoors: hunting equipment, guns, ammo, sporting goods, uniforms, golf clubs, balls, shoes, boots, camping and exercise equipment—you name it. Arthur Gochman, a Harvard law graduate, was a very bright and driven guy, and he owned the stores.

Weekend days were big sale days for Academy. If we prevailed in our lawsuit and closed Academy on Sunday, it would cost Gochman a lot of money.

We filed suit knowing that this time, we would be facing a seasoned opponent. Arthur could afford the best lawyers. He hired his Harvard classmate Ed Cogburn, an accomplished trial lawyer. Judge Richard Millard, a knowledgeable trial judge, heard the case. We had confidence that he would follow the law. He did. Academy Stores were now closed on Sundays.

Ironically, the following Sunday, I needed a propane tank. When I pulled into the Academy parking lot, I realized it was closed—thanks to Bob and me. Arthur's son later sold Academy for millions of dollars. Academy stores are now in sixteen states.

These cases received a great deal of media attention. Every time we had a hearing, all three of Houston's network-affiliated television stations were at the courthouse, along with the *Houston Post* and the *Houston Chronicle*. The *Chronicle* ran a feature story about Linda Addison (a prominent adversary in some of our cases), Bob, me, and our careers. KUHT, the local PBS affiliate, broadcast a program featuring Linda and me debating the Blue Law. We had so much television exposure that for several years after the cases were over, I would see someone who would comment, "I saw you on TV the other night." The power of television.

The next stores we took on were the Handy Dan Home Improvement Centers—a chain of big box stores selling everything for contractors and home handymen, including lumber, tools, and appliances. Handy Dan hired Linda to defend them.

We lost this case. We could not figure out the judge's reasoning, as the appellate case law was solidly with us. Years later, I saw the trial judge who explained his reasoning: He thought the law violated the First Amendment, freedom of religion. Linda never made that argument. The judge pulled that out of thin air.

We appealed the decision. We cited one precedent from the appeals court in El Paso that stands out in my memory. Kitchenware was a prohibited item. The store owner argued that the law was vague. The court wrote, "Even in West Texas, we know what china is."

The Texas Legislature was in session with the senators and state representatives paying close attention to the blue law. With the loss of the Handy Dan case, the legislators hoped the appeals court would agree. That would mean the blue law battle would be over and they could avoid having to cast a vote on keeping or repealing it.

There were many devout churchgoers who thought the blue law was important so that employees could go to church on Sunday. Many members of the legislature wanted to avoid the wrath of those devoutly religious voters. The only problem for the legislature was that we won the appeal. Handy Dan was closed on Sunday, but not for long.

Our appellate victory sounded the death knell for the blue law. Leading the charge for repeal was a newly organized lobbying group: Texans for Blue Law Repeal. Their members included national retailers such as K-Mart, Target, Eckerd Drugs, Revco Drugs, Zales Jewelers, Sears, and the Southland Corp., operator of nearly one thousand 7-Eleven convenience stores in the state. They hired powerful Austin lobbyists. The Houston Retail Merchants Association was no match.

In 1985, the Texas Legislature repealed the blue law.

After the repeal, the swan song for Bob and me was a live interview on Channel 2's six o'clock news. The remote broadcast took place in my living room. Ron Stone, the folksy and popular KPRC anchor, asked us about our take on the repeal. But it was Stone's humor that capped the interview. With so many stores opening and employees working instead of staying home, he remarked, "Well, fellows, I guess that means no more fried chicken on Sunday."

It was quite a run.

Hugh Roy Cullen

Arabesque

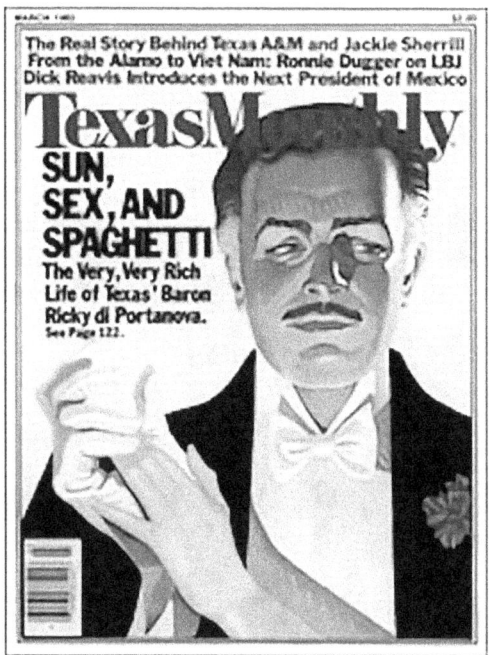

Ricky on the cover of Texas Monthly Magazine

Roy Cohn and Donald Trump

Chief Quanah Parker

The Llano Estacado

Uncle Jack Leaving for World War I, Dad in the Lower Left

Young Florence at the Adolphus Hotel - Dallas

West Texas Cotton Fields

Lamesa Cheerleaders

The Wall

Shamrock Hotel

Thomas R. Conner

Glenn McCarthy Wildcatter

The Houston Press

Settles Hotel Lobby

Midnight Cowboy Listening to Mr. Sunshine

The Phi Psi House

Doris and Bob Angleton

	Mon	Tues	Wed.	Thurs	Fri	C/C	Sat	Sun	Total	Notes
25									0	
42	600	1,180	135	550	515		3,005		2,155	pd
45						200			200	
52			100						100	
53	55		50						5	
59	385	370	145	330	400		2,230	500	3,330	$1050 c/o -1500
67	65	180	20	80			120		55	
122		50	500	550	200	450	550	750	750	
123						45			45	
125	5		50	270		70		45	250	pd
152						110			110	
158						480			480	
162	20	235	360	660			20		825	B
206A	1,400	1,550	165	1,570	760		1,220	1,060	35	
258					50	10	200	150	410	pd
262						120			120	
264	375			115	50			330	20	
271									0	
272					270				270	
274	40	10	65	85	10		30	285	355	B pd
281		800							800	B pd CH
285		110				230		10	110	
295						215			215	
331	1,000	1,000		1,000		650	2,200		1,450	
347						0		200	200	pd
349	290	200	220	30	400			560	80	
356	330	110	20	500	190		20	770	560	pd
357						480			480	
359		5	45	110				110	180	pd
363						430			430	
365	200	1,150	1,150	50			1,150	900	2,400	pd
366			55	110		145			310	
370	160		155	215	50	455	155		450	
376						1,700			1,700	
382						540			540	
386		90	340	120	300		125	175	120	pd
395						35		110	145	
483	1,430	2,230	370	595			410	285	1,720	
491	50	95		10			55		80	pd
544		210				5		100	115	
548						300			300	
552						200			200	
553		105	55	0			535		695	pd 555 c/o -160
557						390			390	
587						220			220	
589						25			25	
590						0		500	500	pd
637		220				60			280	
652	400	960	1,640		960		320	400	840	pd B
653							1,400	2,700	4,100	B pd CH
656						385		550	935	B pd CH
661						10		100	90	
677		440	200	190	300		240	200	690	pd
681	105		50			135	380	50	620	
742		100			100		100		100	
744	330	330	300	50	600		1,110	30	1,370	B pd CH
757	4,695	1,210	340	210	2,730		735	1,205	1,105	B pd B pd 11 mu 9379 9 17/9
785		220	10			100		100	230	
788	1,100	760	480	610	300	30	3,055		4,155	B pd
790	220	90	120	90	200	180	110		250	
792						800			800	15-Jan
832	2,755								2,755	B pd
833	118	155	90	20	259		638	402	50	B pd
834		490	240	1,705	1,930		5	670	4,050	B pd
842	4,850	4,375	10,480	800	10,375		9,775	4,000	14,205	B pd
849			3,500						3,500	B pd
866	4,400	1,800	3,800	1,800	2,200		2,600	4,600	6,400	B pd CH
961	550	170	620	70	300	290	600	330	610	B pd B
985	1,800	4,400	4,000	2,200	3,800		4,400	2,400	5,000	B pd B
D	8,828	8,560	21,260	285	11,461	3,115	4,153	9,543	7,565	

One of Bob's Bookie Sheets

Bob Arrested

Judge Pat Gregory

Princess Grace and Lynn Wyatt

Priscilla and Cullen Davis in happier times

Andrea & Priscilla

Jerry Argovitz with Herschel Walker, Billy Sims, & Marcus Allen

The Emerald Lakes Weminuche Wilderness Area

Emily & President Bush

16

The Bed Rolled Out

DAN KING WAS GENERAL COUNSEL TO St. Luke's and Texas Children's Hospitals. Calling me one day, he asked, "Would you like to do some medical malpractice defense work?"

I was highly complimented. I had never engaged in what was commonly called "insurance defense" cases.

These two hospitals were not ordinary hospitals; they were two flagships of the world-famous Texas Medical Center in Houston. I told Dan I would be honored.

Many of the claims brought against the hospitals were "nuisance cases": those with little merit. Because of the expense the claimant's lawyers faced, primarily hiring medical experts, most of these cases were disposed of before getting close to the courthouse. When I was assigned *Cole v. St. Luke's Hospital*, the facts alleged appeared far from nuisance.

Yvonne Cole was recovering from back surgery as a patient at St. Luke's. One day post-surgery, she got out of bed to use the bathroom. On returning, she sat back on the edge of her bed and the bed rolled out from under her. She violently fell on the floor.

At least that's what her lawsuit contended. She claimed her back was reinjured and now she was suffering terribly.

She hired George Bishop as her lawyer. George's reputation was less than stellar, as he was known for "embellishing" his cases.

We reviewed her medical records. The nurses' notes did not mention the bed roll-out or a fall. In the hospital world, "If it's not charted, it didn't happen." We talked to the nurses. They had no recollection of this event. They also told us that there was no policy in the hospital requiring that the beds' wheels be locked.

Customarily, a party's deposition is taken in the lawyer's office. When I called George to find a convenient time for Yvonne's deposition, he informed me that she was in such terrific pain, she couldn't come downtown. We would have to go to her house.

Arriving there, we were greeted by her husband and George. Entering the living room, there was Yvonne lying on the floor. George explained that her pain was so horrific that the floor was the only place where she found comfort.

In her deposition, she repeated her version of the bed rolling out from under her and how much agony she was suffering. The deposition was videotaped, and she took advantage to grimace at the camera each time she moved, her voice barely audible.

Already believing the case didn't pass the "smell test," I engaged Rob Kimmons, the best private investigator I've ever had.

It was the Saturday after Yvonne's deposition. Rob was at her house early and he followed her as she drove to Randall's Supermarket. She arrived, getting in and out of her car with no apparent difficulty. After some thirty minutes, she returned to her car with a grocery cart crammed with full bags. She unloaded the bags into her SUV, bending over, shoving them in. No problem. No apparent pain.

And all of this was on videotape.

The next day was Sunday. Rob repeated his routine. The family left late morning for the community swimming pool. At the pool, Yvonne was jumping in and out, playing with her children. Rob told me that he was concerned that he would be "burned" while taping her. "I was wearing street clothes," he said, "and didn't look like I belonged there, and I had a video camera taping the pool. My only thought was, 'Yvonne is stupid.'" But we were smart enough to use all of the video tapes at trial, though George hurled every objection imaginable to keep the tapes away from the jury.

George hired a retired registered nurse as his expert witness. We investigated her and learned that she testified on a regular basis for plaintiffs in medical malpractice cases.

All hospitals have numerous policies the staff must follow. In this case, George's nurse testified St. Luke's violated the "standard of care" for hospitals, because St. Luke's did not have a policy to "lock the bed wheels."

My law partner, Steve Lindamood, took the nurse's deposition—and he was prepared. He asked her about the numerous cases that she had testified in as a paid expert, and how many hospitals in the medical center had a policy requiring the beds be locked. She was unsure but said "probably most of them."

Steve pulled out the policies used by four other hospitals in the medical center. Handing the documents to her, he asked her to go through them and find the policy that required their nursing staff to "lock the wheels." She found none.

He then asked her to provide any policies from other hospitals that required bed wheel-locking. "I have some, but not with me." Steve asked her to send them to us after her deposition. We never received any.

We thought that George would want to settle the case and offered him the cost of defense, what the hospital would have to pay us. By now, we viewed this as a "nuisance" case. George made the exorbitant demand of $500,000. The hospital said no.

At trial, our expert witness was Dr. Stan Jones, a noted orthopedic surgeon who specialized in injuries to the spine. He was the orthopedist for the famous Houston Oilers running back Earl Campbell.

Dr. Jones left the witness stand and stood in front of the jury. Like a professor, he explained Yvonne's medical records and placed "before and after" X-rays of her back on the screen. He methodically testified that her injuries before and after "the bed rolling out" were the same—that there was no new injury.

Yes, we won the case.

As for George, he was later convicted of tax evasion and sentenced to three years in prison. The State Bar of Texas disbarred him.

17

The Disbarred Judge

IT WAS SO UNFORTUNATE AND SO PREVENTABLE. A well-respected judge lost his law license and was forced to retire from the bench. All because of $5,000.

Judge Pat Gregory presided over Harris County Probate Court 1 for twenty-three years. He was extremely fair. No one questioned his knowledge of the Texas Probate Code. In fact, he'd written most of it. Jovial off the bench, this hefty jurist wielded aggressive command of his courtroom. Presiding over cases that made the national news, he was fearless in his rulings, which were seldom reversed.

In the 1970s, Judge Gregory presided over cases such as the estate settlement of Candace Mossler, a socialite accused of killing her wealthy husband, the infamous Howard Hughes will contest, and *di Portanova v. Cullen*, earlier described.

Before Pat Gregory's tenure, probate judges spent their time admitting wills to probate, administering the estates of people who died without a will, and appointing guardians for people unable to manage their affairs. The few jury trials they heard usually involved will contests and trustees accused of stealing from their wards.

In rewriting the probate code, Gregory greatly expanded the jurisdiction of Texas probate courts with just a few words. The court now had jurisdiction over "any matter incident to an estate." This meant that cases such as wrongful death—once the exclusive jurisdiction of the more powerful state district courts—could be brought in the probate court where the decedent's estate was pending. If the court was administering a guardianship, any matter relating to the ward's financial estate could be brought in the probate court. That is how *di Portanova v. Cullen* ended up in Gregory's court.

Wayne Fisher, a former president of the state bar and noted plaintiff's attorney, was one of the first to take advantage of the expanded law. He brought a wrongful death claim in Judge Gregory's court. "The district courts have a backlog of cases," Wayne explained. "I can get to trial months faster in probate court."

Another case before Gregory that garnered a great deal of local press was *Wyatt v. Sakowitz*. The society columns had christened Bobby Sakowitz the "Merchant Prince of Houston." His two great-uncles, Simon and Tobias, had sold clothes from pushcarts in Galveston. In 1902, they saved enough money to open a dry goods store. They prospered. When Bobby's father and uncle took over the Galveston store, they moved it to Houston. Tobias's son, Bernard, took control of the store in the '50s. Over the next two decades, the store prospered and grew to four locations in Houston. From the '50s to the '80s, Sakowitz was more exclusive than Neiman Marcus.

Bernard's son Bobby became the store's president in 1968.

Bobby's ambitions were grand, and by 1984, he had opened Sakowitz stores in Amarillo, Scottsdale, Dallas, Midland, and Tulsa. The stores relied on oil-rich customers. Unfortunately, Bobby did not see the oil bust of the mid-80s coming. In 1985,

Sakowitz filed for bankruptcy. This once-great retail empire fell to pieces, and its grand downtown Houston flagship store, its facade covered in marble, became a parking garage.

Bobby's sister Lynn was married to a wealthy Houston oilman, Oscar Wyatt. Their Houston mansion flanked the entrance to the River Oaks Country Club. Lynn threw magnificent parties there and at their second home in the south of France. Celebrities and movie stars often gathered there. Princess Grace of Monaco was one of Lynn's closest friends. *Vanity Fair* and *Town and Country* magazines wrote stories about her parties, jewels, wardrobe, and homes. And Oscar hated Bobby Sakowitz.

Oscar believed Bobby ran the stores into the ground and in the process embezzled profits that rightfully belonged to the trusts for his and Lynn's sons. No doubt Bobby had "borrowed" money from these funds. Yet at the time the suit was brought, he had fully repaid the funds with interest.

In 1990, at Oscar's insistence, his and Lynn's son—Bobby's nephew—Douglas Wyatt sued Bobby, seeking $7.5 million in damages. The suit was filed in Pat Gregory's court.

The two-week jury trial resulted in a verdict in favor of Bobby.

Wyatt filed a motion for a new trial, asking Gregory to throw out the verdict and retry the case. Post-trial, a noted probate lawyer in Houston pointed out that Gregory had made a fundamental error. When he instructed the jury, he'd placed the burden of proof on Wyatt to prove that Bobby did something wrong. But the law says that when a trustee is sued—which in this case was Bobby—it's the trustee's job to prove that he did nothing wrong. Gregory properly granted a new trial. David Berg, Bobby's lawyer, was not happy with the ruling reversing his victory. Before the case could be retried, Gregory was indicted for tax evasion.

One of Gregory's sons was in criminal trouble. Gregory needed money to help him hire a lawyer. A $5,000 donation was made to the Texas College of Probate Judges. Gregory was its sitting president. But Gregory bypassed the association; he put the money in his personal account.

Gregory was never sure how the federal prosecutor knew of the $5,000, but he had his suspicions. Whether true or not, Gregory believed Berg used his influence to get the US attorney to investigate him, resulting in the criminal charges.

No doubt he got the money. No doubt he wrongfully kept it. No doubt he failed to report it. He settled his criminal case for a plea bargain of one year in federal prison—Three Rivers in South Texas, reserved for nonviolent offenders.

On arriving at Three Rivers, the warden noted who Gregory was. It was rare that a former judge became a guest of the federal government. During a conversation about his prison work assignment, Gregory informed the warden of his success in using the newest computer technology, streamlining the probate court's record-keeping. Gregory went to work for the warden, upgrading the prison's record-keeping using the same computer knowledge he'd gained as a judge.

When Gregory's sentence was completed, the warden offered him a job: move to Three Rivers and keep working for the prison system. When Gregory told me this story, he laughed. "The one place I never wanted to see again was Three Rivers."

In February 2002, my phone rang.

"Top Cat, Pat Gregory here." Gregory always referred to me as Top Cat, an obvious play on my initials. "I want to have lunch with you." Over lunch, he said, "I want to get my law license back. I want you to represent me."

I was both honored and concerned. The honor was that Pat Gregory knew many great trial lawyers, among them Joe Jamail and Wayne Fisher. They and a host of others would gladly represent him. My concern was that this would be a very tough case. The Republicans had taken over the courthouse. It would be a trial before a Republican judge, not a jury. Gregory was a lifelong and well-known Democrat.

We hope that all judges are fair and unbiased. For the most part, that's true. But Texas judges are elected. They are political animals. They run as Democrats and Republicans. Giving a de-frocked Democratic judge his law license back would be an unpopular decision among Republicans, no matter that it might be the right thing to do.

On July 15, 2002, trial in *The State Bar of Texas v. Kenneth Pat Gregory* commenced. We were in the 55th Judicial District Court, one of the oldest District Courts in Harris County, established in 1897. Presiding over the bench was who we lawyers refer to as a "baby judge." Jeff Brown was a new, young Republican judge, coming from the large, conservative law firm Baker and Botts.

My first witness was William Miller, a partner at Andrews Kurth, another large Houston firm. Among the firm's and Miller's clients were the Howard Hughes estate and the Hughes heirs. Miller was considered the dean of Houston probate lawyers. No doubt Judge Brown knew his reputation.

As I did with all witnesses, I went through his background, education, practice experience, and the legal honors awarded him, which were numerous. I also established that Gregory was the father of the modern Texas Probate Code, that he had years of experience on the bench, and that he was a fair, good judge.

After acknowledging that Gregory should never have taken the $5,000, I asked, "Despite that theft, do you believe that Pat Gregory is a man of integrity and honesty?"

"Yes, Pat Gregory is a man of integrity and honesty," he emphatically stated.

"If his law license is reinstated, do you have an opinion as to the contributions he would make as a lawyer?"

"Absolutely," Miller said. "He would be hired by other lawyers and law firms to help them. His knowledge is extraordinary."

"Do you believe the court should restore his license?" I asked.

"Without a doubt."

My next witness was Judge Guy Herman, the presiding probate judge in Texas. He extolled Gregory's many accomplishments and contributions to the probate code and system in Texas. He enthusiastically endorsed our request.

Then, Judge Russell Austin, a Republican judge of Harris County Probate Court 3, likewise praised Gregory's accomplishments and urged that his law license be reinstated.

In addition, two former presidents of the State Bar of Texas and a former president of the Houston Bar Association testified, agreeing with our other witnesses.

Next, coming from Pontiac, Michigan, was Probate Judge Barry Grant. Judge Grant, in his career, had served as president of the Michigan Probate Judges Association, the National Council of Juvenile and Family Court Judges, and the Children's Charter of the Courts of Michigan. He and Gregory had worked closely together on continuing legal education for probate judges. After he verified the testimony of the other witnesses, I asked my last question. "Who paid your expenses to come to Houston from Michigan?"

"I did," Judge Grant said.

My opposing counsel was Jennifer Hasly, a three-year lawyer working in the General Counsel's office of the State Bar of Texas. Her cross-examination strategy for all the witnesses was to have them agree that Gregory, taking the $5,000 was unthinkable for a lawyer, much less a judge. Jennifer had her ammunition. She fired it repeatedly.

On her cross examination, our witnesses stuck to their guns. What Gregory did was wrong. They also agreed he paid a very high price for this mistake, and he should get his law license back.

My last witness was Pat Gregory.

My intent was to avoid having Gregory blow his own horn. I had already employed an entire orchestra for that. After giving a brief background about his education and career, we went to the heart of the problem.

"What you did, in taking that $5,000 and not reporting it, was a violation of your oath as a lawyer and as a judge, was it not?" I asked.

"Absolutely," Gregory said.

"What is the price that you paid for that act?"

"I lost my law license. I resigned from a bench I sat on for twenty-three years. I spent a year in prison." His voice was choking. "Worst of all things, I hurt my family, I ruined my reputation, and I am sorry and ashamed."

"Pass the witness," I concluded.

Jennifer had reloaded with the same ammunition. When she concluded, both sides rested, and we made our final arguments.

The court spoke. "Counsel, I will take this under advisement and fax my ruling to you tomorrow."

I knew then we had lost.

The evidence was straightforward. If he was going to rule for Judge Gregory, he would say it then. I turned to Gregory and said, "He doesn't have the cojones to rule for us."

I returned to my office an hour later. Evidently, Judge Brown had no need to wait until the next day to fax his decision. I was in my office for less than fifteen minutes when a fax came in. "Petitioner's Request to Reinstate Law License is Denied."

It was evident that an hour earlier, Judge Brown did not have the courage to look Gregory in the eye and tell him that.

I called my client and gave him the bad news. Among other comments, Gregory said, "I'm not surprised. We gave it a good shot." He concluded, "Top Cat, you did a super job. You are my friend. Thank you."

As for the players in this drama:

Gregory was hired by numerous law firms as a "paralegal," who advised them as to their probate litigation.

Judge Brown was later appointed by Governor Rick Perry as a Texas Supreme Court Justice. Subsequently, President Donald Trump appointed him a federal district judge in Galveston.

Jennifer Hasly was elected president of the Houston Bar Association in 2021 and enjoys a stellar reputation representing lawyers accused of malfeasance by the State Bar.

As for Bobby and the Wyatts, the case was never retried. They settled. The terms are confidential.

Pat Gregory died of heart failure in 2011.

18

The Worst Day of My Law Practice

WE WERE HOLDING AN EXXON STOCK CERTIFICATE worth $500,000 in escrow in our firm's safe deposit box. Our client, Mr. Eliot, and his daughter had a dispute over the rightful ownership of the stock. We successfully resolved the matter in his favor. It was time to retrieve the certificate and return it to Mr. Eliot.

Approaching our office manager, Barbara Bland, I asked her to go to the bank, open the safe deposit box, and get the certificate. She and I were the only ones with access to the box. She looked at me with a quizzical expression. "I took Clement over there several months ago, and he took the certificate. He said those were your instructions."

Poor Barbara appeared physically ill when she figured out that she had been duped.

Clement Williams had been our law clerk for two years. J.P. and I were pleased with his work effort and intelligence. When he passed the bar, we hired him as an associate attorney. He had been practicing law with us for a year when he decided that theft was a superior calling.

We soon determined what had happened with this bit of larceny. Clement stole the certificate and managed to cash it in. By the time we found out, he had taken a trip to New York and bought a new car as well as a small beach house in Galveston.

The first thing I did was call the client and tell him what happened. That was a difficult but necessary phone call. I assured him that he would be made whole. He was a former trustee of Rice University and a successful, retired businessman. I was grateful as he was kind and understanding. Fortunately, we had bonded our employees, and we were able to repay Mr. Eliot within a matter of weeks. The insurance carrier took over Clement's beach house and car.

The next items of business: get Clement charged with theft and get him disbarred. We filed a complaint with the State Bar and filed criminal charges of theft with the district attorney's office. A warrant was issued for Clement's arrest.

Once his mother learned of the warrant, she went into action, checking him into a mental hospital. She must have believed that would keep him out of jail. When the deputies arrived to arrest him, they were told by the hospital that he could not be released. Naturally, the deputies were reluctant to barge into a hospital.

Thankfully, we were friends with the district attorney, Johnny Holmes. When we learned of the hospital roadblock, we called Johnny, who called the sheriff. "I don't care about some private hospital telling us what to do," Holmes said. "You have a warrant signed by a judge. Pick him up."

And they did.

While all of this was playing out over several weeks, I ran into a lady whom I knew from previous litigation. I had not seen Judy Rives for several years and asked where she was working. "For the sheriff's office," she said. "I am the manager of the county jail." As I told her the saga of Clement and how he would soon be arrested, she volunteered, "When he's picked up, he'll be put in general population."

General population in the Harris County jail was overcrowded and dangerous. There were four prisoners in a cell; during the daytime, all the prisoners would mingle with each other and take their meals together. Many of these prisoners had been charged with violent crimes. They were rough and tough. Clement was a heavyset, rather effeminate young man. General population would be unpleasant for him.

His mother could not afford to make bond, so Clement sat in the county jail for four months before his case was called to trial. J.P. and I, along with our entire staff, were in the courtroom when Clement was brought in. Having not seen him for all those months, we found his appearance alarming—he'd shrunk in size, having lost a great deal of weight; his eyes and cheeks were gaunt; and he had dark bags under his eyes. Not a lot of imagination was required to know that Clement had not enjoyed his time in general population.

The assistant DA made a plea bargain for Clement to plead guilty to theft, his sentence being time served and the surrender of his law license. We thought we would never hear about Clement again.

Fast forward twenty-five years to a small item in the *Houston Chronicle*: "Hospital Purchaser Pleads Guilty to Theft." Somehow, Clement had landed a job with St. Luke's Episcopal Hospital and rose in the ranks to the level of being able to approve expenditures for hospital purchases. He formed dummy companies, billed the hospital for phony expenses, and authorized payments to his dummy companies—to the tune of $2 million. This time, the plea deal was five years in a federal penitentiary. Tigers don't change their stripes. Neither did Clement.

When we first learned of his theft in our office, we were concerned he might have stolen from other clients. Hiring an independent auditor to examine our books, we were relieved to find that his theft was limited to the stock certificate—with one exception. Anne and I had invested in a small gas well some years back and had been receiving monthly royalty checks. Clement evidently went through the mail and, each time a check came in, he took it and forged our names. The total take was less than $500.

19

The Richest Man Ever Tried for Murder

"THE MANSION," AS IT WAS KNOWN, COVERED almost 19,000 square feet atop a knoll on 181 acres abutting the Colonial Country Club in Fort Worth, Texas. The stark white structure, with an indoor swimming pool and priceless art, was more a museum than a home. The only ones in the house were Priscilla Davis and me. We were sitting around the kitchen island. It was a late spring night in 1979.

"Stan and I came in the back door. He went up the back stairs to the master bedroom. I went into the kitchen. I noticed the door to the basement was open and the stairwell light was on. I went to close the door and noticed blood was smeared down the side wall of the stairwell."

Priscilla was telling me about the night of August 2, 1976, when her estranged husband, Cullen Davis, murdered her twelve-year-old daughter (Cullen's stepdaughter), Andrea, as well as Priscilla's boyfriend, Stan Farr, and shot Priscilla herself.

Cullen Davis was the wealthy heir of an oil empire. Priscilla, his second wife, grew up in Galena Park, Texas. Author Gary Cartwright described Priscilla as "a sexy platinum blonde who came so far from the other side of the tracks that it wasn't even on the same railroad." Striking, usually wearing low-cut blouses showing off her majestic breast implants, she seldom removed the diamond necklace sparkling with the words "Rich Bitch."

My involvement with Priscilla Davis began with a phone call. The caller identified himself as David Clayton. "I'm Priscilla Davis's brother, and I'm helping her find new lawyers." Their divorce had made national headlines—not for the divorce, but because Cullen was the richest man ever tried for murder.

They had been married for four years when he built The Mansion. Costing $6 million for the construction—$39 million in 2024 dollars—it included five bedrooms, eleven baths, an indoor pool, courtyard, balconies, tunnels, and over one hundred oil paintings and art objects.

Early during the divorce proceedings, Priscilla was awarded exclusive use of the house, along with hefty support payments. And Cullen was ordered not to come near it—or her.

With Cullen out of the house, Priscilla moved in her latest boyfriend, a motorcycle "biker," and turned The Mansion into a party house—a party that would last for nine months. During that time, a variety of characters, musicians, and drug dealers drifted in and out, some living there for weeks at a time.

On August 2, 1976, Cullen returned to court asking for the return of The Mansion. Instead, his request was not only denied, but he was ordered to increase his support payments to Priscilla. He was livid.

That was the night of horror that Priscilla would tell me about. Cullen would murder Priscilla's twelve-year-old daughter, shoot Priscilla, murder her boyfriend, Stan Farr, and would shoot and paralyze a young man named Gus Gavrel.

Three eyewitnesses would identify Cullen Davis as the attacker.

In the early morning hours of the next day, Cullen Davis was arrested and charged with capital murder.

Because of pretrial publicity, the trial was moved to Amarillo. Author Gary Cartwright quoted one local philosopher describing Amarillo as "a place where they send their daughters east to be educated and keep their sons at home to learn how to be bastards like their daddies." The perfect place to try Cullen Davis.

Cullen hired a group of well-known criminal defense lawyers, led by Houston's Richard "Racehorse" Haynes. I knew Race and had watched him in action. He was always prepared and meticulous. Haynes's trial strategy to get Cullen off was to the point: "I'm going to try Priscilla."

And he did.

Priscilla was on the stand for eleven days, six of those days being cross-examined by Haynes. Good to his word, he grilled her about the nine-month party and the riff-raff that drifted in and out, some even using their own keys provided by Priscilla. Testimony also showed that Stan's life was threatened by a former partner and brought out facts about her drug and alcohol habits. Race then took the Fort Worth Police Department to task for its sloppy crime scene investigation. The prosecution called twenty-three witnesses; the defense, forty-four. Jury selection began on June 27, 1977, and the jury began deliberations on November 17—the longest murder trial in Texas history.

Cullen was found not guilty. After the trial, some jurors said they believed Cullen was guilty, but the judge's instructions were that in order to find a "guilty" verdict, their decision must be based on a *"reasonable and moral certainty."* They said the prosecution failed to meet that burden.

After the trial, one of the prosecutors said, "I never thought I would say this, but it seems we have two systems of justice in this country: one for the rich and one for the poor."

My partner, James Patrick Smith, and I agreed to take Priscilla's case. At the DFW Airport, we were met by her driver, James McDaniel. James had been with Priscilla from the time she came home from the hospital, recuperating from her gunshot wound.

Arriving at The Mansion, we entered through the rear entry into the kitchen and met Priscilla Davis. She was tiny by any standard, with platinum blonde hair, wearing a short skirt and a blouse that failed to adequately contain her famous breast implants. Of course, she was wearing the "Rich Bitch" necklace.

Priscilla had suffered through an emotional roller coaster for months: her daughter and boyfriend were murdered; she was shot, almost losing her life; she'd been through a protracted divorce; she was cross-examined for days by Haynes during Cullen's trial; then she was devastated by the not guilty verdict. Now she was on the eve of her divorce being finalized and had lost confidence in her lawyers.

We explained to her what she already knew. The evidence in the divorce case had already been presented in court. The only remaining element was to submit the legal positions of both sides to the judge, along with final argument, which her lawyers were already preparing. We couldn't put the genie back in the bottle.

Her comment: "You don't know Cullen Davis. Once the divorce is over, there will be more problems. Cullen hates me. I have to have new lawyers to get me through whatever comes next."

We also explained to her that once we notified her present lawyers that we were coming in, they would be resentful of us looking over their shoulders. She said, "Great. That'll make 'em nervous. Maybe they'll do a better job."

Jerry Lucas and Ron Anderson were two journeymen lawyers. Both were solo practitioners, who—like many such lawyers—took a variety of cases such as divorce, criminal, DWI, and personal injury. When Priscilla hired them, it was on the recommendation of a friend. It was the first time she had ever hired a lawyer.

Before meeting Priscilla, we examined many of the court records and the lawyers' billings. Each August, the State Bar sponsors a weeklong seminar for family lawyers. It is intensive in training trial tactics, providing updates on cases and new laws, and covering every topic that touches family law. Both attorneys had attended the seminar, and—surprising to us—billed her for their continuing legal education.

Cullen's divorce lawyer was Donn Fullenweider, who was from Houston as we were. Donn was Haynes's partner, a premiere family lawyer in Texas, and a consummate professional. Over the years, I would have many cases with Donn. We were always congenial adversaries—he was gracious enough to sponsor my nomination to the American Academy of Matrimonial Lawyers.

Priscilla notified Lucas and Anderson that we would be substituting as her attorneys as soon as the judge entered the final orders in the divorce. They were in the process of finalizing their written arguments to the judge on the various issues in the case. We reviewed their work product and made recommendations.

We were surprised that they'd assigned a legal secretary to draft some arguments. She knew no law and her drafting was purely emotional: "Poor Priscilla … a woman needs her home … she's suffered enough," and similar pleas. We knew these were nonstarters with any judge. We were correct. The issues she'd championed were denied.

Judge Clyde Ashworth was a decorated Marine in the Pacific Theater in World War II. The first time I saw him in court, my thoughts were "This is a good judge." He had a calm judicial demeanor. He was courteous to all counsel and litigants and thoughtfully listened to all arguments. Unlike some judges, his ego did not dominate the courtroom.

There would be several hearings before Judge Ashworth prior to the official entry of the final divorce decree. Priscilla wanted us there for each one. Though the working relationship with Lucas and Anderson was tense, they did consult with us on the final matters. When Judge Ashworth entered his rulings, we were able to make drafting suggestions on the final orders.

Though she'd hired both J.P. and me, there was often no need for two attorneys to go to Fort Worth. As it worked out, I was the one to make most of the trips. Being together a lot, I coined her nickname "PD." I would call her that for the rest of her life.

After her ordeals, most of her "friends" proved to be the fair-weather variety—they abandoned her. She began to rely on me for much of her everyday matters, such as meeting with her insurance agent and her real estate agent. There were also the matters of finalizing her dealings with Lucas and Anderson and just giving her basic advice on how to get on with her life. No doubt she was tough, but after all that occurred, she felt alone and frightened—and convinced that Cullen would try to kill her again.

To show me that she was not the only one who feared Cullen, she took me to his brother Bill's palatial home in the exclusive River Crest neighborhood. Because of Cullen's greed and attempts to take over Bill's portion of the business, he and Bill had a series of ongoing and extremely bitter lawsuits.

Entering the kitchen, Priscilla introduced me to Mitzi, Bill's wife. They led me to a side room. On entering, an armed guard was sitting before a bank of television monitors. Cameras from all over the yard and each side of the house were blinking above them. Mitzi explained to me that they kept armed guards on the property, twenty-four hours a day, seven days a week. There was no doubt that Cullen's not guilty verdict failed to assuage their fears.

While in Fort Worth, I would stay in a guest room in The Mansion. Priscilla and I were in the kitchen one night around 9 p.m., sitting around the island, drinking a glass of wine, when she said, "I want to walk you through that night." Of course, I knew what "that night" was.

The basement door was just off the kitchen. She showed me where she'd found a bloody handprint. "I knew whoever was here would want me to walk down those stairs, so he could shoot me."

Walking back through the kitchen, she pointed at the laundry room door. "That's where Cullen walked out. He had the maid's Afro wig on his head with his hand in a plastic bag. It was so strange. He said 'Hi' like we were just bumping into each other. We weren't ten feet apart. He pulled the trigger. I was shot in the chest and fell. I heard Stan coming down the stairs. Cullen shot him and Stan fell next to me. I could hear another gunshot, the one that Cullen fired to make sure Stan was dead. He must have thought I was dead because he left. I crawled and was able to get out through the breakfast room door and got behind some thick bushes. Then I saw Cullen coming back. Just as he started looking around for me, I heard a car pull up. That's when he left again."

Gus Gavrel and Bev Bass were friends of Dee, Priscilla's oldest daughter. They came to the house because they thought Dee was there. Cullen would shoot Gus and paralyze him. Bev was able to flee.

Priscilla continued: "I started stumbling, crawling down the hill to the neighborhood closest to us. At the first house, I managed to get to the front door and started pounding on it. A couple came to the door but wouldn't open it. I was crying, pleading. 'Please help me. I'm Priscilla Davis, I live in the big house up on the hill.' The EMTs and police showed up. My only thought was, 'I'm safe for now.'"

The jury may have found Cullen Davis not guilty, but that night I was convinced "to a moral certainty" that Cullen Davis had killed Andrea and Stan, and that he'd shot Priscilla and Gus.

The judge's final orders gave Cullen The Mansion, finding it was his separate property. Priscilla was ordered to vacate the residence on a hot August night in 1979, then Cullen could reclaim it. My job was to get Priscilla out and hand the keys over to Cullen. She and I were alone, except for one other person, a reporter from *People* magazine.

Priscilla had been on the cover of *People* once and she thoroughly enjoyed the publicity. It was a picture of her with a pistol in an ankle holster. The reporter showed zero interest when I told her she needed to leave. As a matter of fact, neither did PD.

Cullen would be at the house at midnight, and a confrontation with him was not at the top of my agenda. As midnight approached, I insisted that the reporter leave. We were under a court order. Finally, at midnight, I succeeded in getting her out of the house. As the reporter pulled out, Cullen pulled in. In a demanding voice, he asked, "Is she gone?"

"No," I replied, "She'll be out soon."

Cullen reminded me that she was ordered out of the house at midnight. At this point, my patience was thin. "Cullen, I know what the order says. She will be out tonight."

"Okay," he said, "I'll be back in thirty minutes." By the time he returned, Priscilla had left the house. I handed Cullen the house keys and drove off.

Cullen spent the next few days going through the house to categorize any items that might be missing or that he believed had been damaged.

We were now Priscilla's attorneys of record, and we were soon served with a motion for contempt and a motion for damages based on Cullen's claims.

On the morning of the resultant hearing, we picked up PD at her rental house. The day before, I'd cautioned her to dress very conservatively. When she walked downstairs, she looked lovely, wearing a brown skirt that came to her knees and a matching brown jacket, beneath which was a sheer beige blouse with a bow at the throat. This was the most conservative I had ever seen her dress.

As James pulled the limo into the street, she unbuttoned her jacket and opened it. She wore no bra, and her breasts and nipples could clearly be seen.

I didn't take two seconds.

"James," I said firmly, "turn the car around. We're going back to the house."

To PD, I said, "I want you to put on a bra."

She reluctantly agreed.

When she came back to the car, I said, "Let me see."

She unbuttoned her jacket. Still no bra, but she had put band-aids over her nipples.

"That's all you're getting, Tom, but I'll leave the jacket buttoned."

Our case was the only one on Judge Ashworth's docket. Fullenweider proceeded with his motions, having Cullen testify as to his various complaints, introducing photographs to memorialize his damage claims.

Our response: "No questions, your honor."

We then moved to dismiss all of Cullen's motions. A divorce decree had been entered. It was a final order. If Cullen had any complaints, he should have brought them before entry of the decree. His lawyer's contention: "Judge, there was no way he could know of the damage. He didn't have access to the house until after the decree was signed."

My response: "Judge, he could have filed a motion to inspect the property before the decree was entered. He's been quoted in the paper saying that he was worried about what Mrs. Davis had done to the house. If he was that concerned, he should have asked his lawyers to get him in."

After listening to all arguments, Judge Ashworth announced, "The motion to dismiss is granted." Priscilla was giddy. She was used to either losing or being beaten up on cross-examination. This time she had a win, prompting her to remark, "I wish I had you guys a long time ago."

Priscilla was awarded $7 million in cash, much less than the $26 million she'd asked for. Her award would be $40 million in today's dollars. In a letter I sent her early in our representation, I wrote, "*You MUST protect your money and invest it wisely. To do otherwise might find you penniless in a few years.*"

After the divorce award, I told her, "PD, you're a wealthy woman now. You can be fixed for the rest of your life."

I advised her that she should place the money with a competent financial consultant, someone experienced in investing wealth. I warned her that there would be many people trying to get her money in some form, either some wild investment scheme or a stockbroker who would "churn" her account for commissions. She asked me to help her.

My first thought was of Rudge Allen, senior vice president with Fayez Sarofim and Company in Houston. At that time, Sarofim had $15 billion under management, taking care of wealthy individuals, large pension funds, corporate investments, and foundations.

PD flew to Houston to meet Rudge. Sitting in my office the afternoon she arrived, she was obviously in a great deal of pain, a result of the old wound courtesy of Cullen. She said she had run out of Percodan, a drug that she'd admitted an addiction to when cross-examined in the murder trial.

Some six months before, I had the pleasure of a kidney stone, the absolute worst pain in my life. My doctor prescribed Percodan, one of the strongest opioids available. There were only two occasions that I reached for a Percodan. Never has a drug affected me like Percodan. Once the drug took effect, I no longer had any pain, nor would I care if someone had told me that I was broke, my wife had left me, or I had been disbarred. No problem! Yes, it was a very potent narcotic.

In my desk drawer, I had four Percodan left.

"Here you go, PD," I said, handing the bottle to her. The miraculous appearance of the Percodan may have been the most impressive service she believed I ever rendered for her.

I invited her to dinner at our house. She arrived about five and immediately lay down on the living room sofa, the pain still affecting her, the Percodan not much help.

Our daughter Emily was two years old at the time. She immediately crawled up and lay down next to "P'see-yah," as Emily would call her. PD put her arms around Emily. About that time, our Labrador retriever came up to the couch and laid his head next to her. The child and the dog did not move.

Going through my mind: This woman has been accused of horrible things from her biker-drug days, but this child and this dog sense someone entirely different. As PD often told me, "I've done some bad things, but I never murdered a twelve-year-old girl."

The next morning, we went to Rudge's office. Fayez Sarofim, the founder of the company, was a noted art collector. When we walked into the offices, it was like walking into a fine art museum. He had art dating through three centuries. On Fayez's death, the Museum of Fine Arts–Houston held a special exhibit of his collection.

Rudge explained to PD that her funds would be invested in a variety of stocks, some for growth, some for income, while other funds would be placed in bonds and other securities. He related to her the history of the company's performance over thirty years, which was impressive.

We walked out of the office. Her first comment: "He's not flashy enough for me."

My response: "PD, the last thing you want is a flashy money manager. You're not hiring a show pony."

She left Houston and called me a few days later. "I've got some other money guys here in Fort Worth I want you to meet."

The Fort Worth Club is a twelve-story downtown edifice. Founded in 1885, it is the social epicenter of the city. It has fine dining, a ballroom, meeting rooms, guest rooms, workout facilities, and a spa. After Priscilla moved out of The Mansion, I stayed there on my trips to Fort Worth.

Priscilla had three potential "money managers" for me to meet. With appointments arranged for the afternoon, she met me at the Fort Worth Club for lunch. I waited for her in the main dining room, which was packed with businesspeople, attorneys, and "ladies who lunch."

On this cold January day, she swept into the dining room in a full-length mink. Every head in the room turned. Everyone recognized Priscilla Davis.

I helped her remove her coat. She was wearing a denim mini skirt, a T-shirt, no bra, and—of course—the Rich Bitch necklace. Perhaps it was my imagination, but I swear there were audible gasps from some of the women. I remarked, "PD, you never cease to amaze me."

She laughed and said, "Let 'em enjoy the show."

We met with her potential "money managers." They were all stockbrokers, not financial consultants. It took less than thirty minutes with each of them for me to know that none had the ability to manage such a large amount of money. I told Priscilla that Rudge was her best choice. If she didn't like him, I offered to find other competent advisers for her to interview. She said she would stew on it.

Not hearing from PD for a couple of weeks, I called to check on her. She immediately said, "I've found the right guy." She explained that this fellow would invest in antique Rolls-Royces, sterling silver, and other "stuff that he says will grow in value and I can make a lot of money."

I silently groaned to myself. Without success, I did my best to talk her out of this decision. I knew how this movie would end.

About ten years later, I was sitting in my office when PD called.

"Tom, I'm at the Houston airport trying to fly back to Fort Worth. My credit card has been declined." Immediately I said, "Put the agent on the phone and I'll take care of it." After giving the agent my credit card, PD and I chatted for a few minutes and said goodbye.

That was the last time I talked to her.

As of this writing in 2024, Cullen Davis is 90 years old. During the oil bust of the mid-80s, he lost his fortune, became a "born-again Christian," and now lives in a modest home in Fort Worth.

In 2019, The Mansion and the 181 acres it sits on were bought by a developer. The house that held so many ghosts and heartaches fell to the wrecking ball.

In 2001, Priscilla Davis died of breast cancer at the age of 59. At the time of her death, she was living in a one-bedroom apartment in Dallas.

Thomas R. Conner

20

You Can't Win 'Em All

THERE WAS SNOW ON THE GROUND WHEN the trial started in Denton, Texas. When the verdict came in, it was 93 degrees. This would be a long and difficult case.

Emma Carson went to the Denton Regional Medical Center, Denton's largest hospital, to have her baby—a routine event. Ava Allison was in the operating room at the head of the table with Emma. Ava was a certified registered nurse anesthetist—a nurse trained to administer anesthesia, commonly referred to as a CRNA. Dr. Clark, the obstetrician, was present to deliver the baby via C-section.

After Ava injected the anesthetic drug into Emma's vein, something went terribly wrong. Emma suffered a severe allergic reaction. Her throat was swollen shut. She quit breathing. Ava hurriedly inserted a curved tube down Emma's throat to restore her airway, a procedure called "intubation." When Ava completed the intubation, Emma had been without air for several minutes.

When she awakened, she had a healthy baby girl and the mind of a twelve-year-old. The cause: oxygen deprivation. A lawsuit was filed against the hospital on Emma's behalf by her husband, Jimmy, for him individually and on behalf of their baby girl, Sandra. The lawsuit sought $20 million. We were hired to defend the hospital.

In Texas, the law requires that if a CRNA is administering anesthesia, there must be a medical doctor present for supervision. The MD supervisor does not have to be in the operating room, but must be in the operating area, where they can easily be called upon. It is common practice in many hospitals that the surgeon in the operating room, such as Dr. Clark, is the CRNA supervisor.

The hospital had a problem. A month before Emma suffered her tragic event, all the surgeons signed a joint letter to the hospital administrator. They stated in definite terms that they were not supervising the CRNAs. They demanded that an anesthesiologist be physically present in the operating suites if a CRNA was providing the anesthesia. The surgeons would no longer have that responsibility. Dr. Clark's signature was the first on the letter.

Dr. Doug Price was the anesthesiologist who was supposed to be supervising the CRNAs when Emma had her baby. At the time Emma suffered her allergic reaction, he was not in the operating suites. He was not in the hospital. He was driving around Denton in his new Porsche convertible.

This was a challenging case. As we studied the medical records, interviewed Ava and other hospital staff, and engaged our expert witnesses, we thought the case was defensible, though the hospital was very much at risk.

Intubation is a difficult procedure. The patient's head must be cocked backward and the intubation tube must be inserted, something difficult to achieve when the patient has a completely swollen throat. The standard of care says the procedure should not exceed five minutes, as death can occur then. The timeframe in which the lack of oxygen can cause brain damage is variable and cannot be pinpointed.

Based on our expert's evaluation of Ava's performance and Emma's post-operative condition, it was estimated that the intubation took less than three minutes. He would testify Ava met the "standard of care." Of course, Emma's lawyer had an expert anesthesiologist. His opinion was the exact opposite. Ava failed to meet the standard of care in timely inserting the intubation tube.

This case was an exhausting experience because of the travel and living and working in a hotel for ten weeks. My partner Steve Lindamood, our paralegal Jayne Cole, and I decamped to Denton. At the DoubleTree hotel, we took one end of the fifth floor, with five rooms: one for each of us, one for John Teague, the Fort Worth lawyer representing Dr. Price, and one for files and Jayne's word processing equipment.

Our routine: Fly to Dallas Love Field every Sunday night, get in our rent-a-van, and drive to Denton thirty miles away. We were there until the following Friday, trying the case each day and spending our evenings preparing for the next day's witnesses. The judge dismissed court at noon on Friday and we would return to Houston for the weekend.

Judge Harry Klein was a nice man. Too nice. Many times, when there was an objection or argument, he would call all the lawyers into his chambers and allow us to "vent" as much as we wanted—a huge waste of judicial time. This was not customary behavior for a trial judge. Usually, a judge rules promptly from the bench.

No doubt this was a big case, and it intimidated Judge Klein. Seasoned judges would set a time limit at the start of trial. "Gentlemen, you have two weeks to try this case. Each side gets forty hours. I'll keep the time." Not this case.

Both sides rested, final arguments were made, and the jury retired. After two days of deliberation, they returned with their verdict. The hospital was liable and would pay $14 million in damages. Several jurors singled Steve and me out: "You guys are good lawyers and tried a good case. You just had bad facts."

What frustrated us was the reluctance of the hospital's parent company to make a good-faith effort to settle the case. We were confident before trial that the case could settle between $5 million and $7 million. The hospital's only offer was $500,000. The family's lawyers did not bother with a counteroffer.

We later learned that the hospital was for sale. The parent company had no desire for potential buyers to see a balance sheet minus $7 million. They could just list the Denton case as a "matter pending" in their claims department.

The hospital appealed the case. Two years later, the appellate court found no error. The hospital would have to pay.

As for me, when we returned to Houston after the trial concluded, my only thought: "I don't have to go to Denton next week."

21

The Shyster Lawyer

GRACE KING WAS A NAÏVE NINETEEN-YEAR-OLD YOUNG lady when her father died unexpectedly. A widower, he left his entire estate to Grace. She hired a lawyer to probate her father's will. His name was Carl Baker.

Carl, in his late thirties, was handsome and beguiling. The father's will was straightforward. It took little effort on Carl's part to probate the will, and it took little effort on Carl's part to get Grace in his bed.

The estate, now Grace's property, consisted of seventeen oil paintings and two valuable parcels of real estate in Houston. The first real estate holding was a 100-acre tract adjacent to Beltway 8, an outer loop that circles Houston. The second parcel was a five-acre corner lot on Jensen Drive, a major street in east Houston. This property would later be sold for a strip shopping center. At the time of trial, the real estate was valued at more than $3 million.

Trusting her lawyer's pillow talk was a disaster for Grace. "I have some papers you need to sign to finish up your dad's estate," remarked Carl one night. She signed the documents as instructed.

Carl, with a stroke of a pen, was now the owner of Grace's real estate. Grace also signed a mutual release under the guise of a settlement of attorney's fees. Carl's true purpose: Her signature forgave him of any wrongdoing, like him taking her land.

Her romance with Carl was over soon after his chicanery. A year later, with the help of a new boyfriend, Grace determined her unfortunate predicament. She hired me to recover her property. I sued Carl for everything I could think of: fraud, rescission of the deeds, undue influence, legal malpractice, and breach of fiduciary duty—he had done all of those things.

Carl's defense was that the probate was over, he was no longer her lawyer, she signed a release, and she was an adult responsible for knowing what she signed.

The case was tried before a jury over five days. Carl, as we say in lawyer jargon, was an excellent testifier. He sounded convincing to the jury. Grace testified that she had been in love with Carl. She trusted him completely. Because he was her attorney, she felt no need to read the documents he'd asked her to sign.

I called six lawyers and a sitting probate court judge as experts to testify to Carl's misdeeds—that he had charged unreasonable fees, that he defrauded her and breached his duty to Grace as her attorney.

In a surprise move, Carl called as an expert witness former Harris County judge Bob Wilson, who had been voted out of office two years before. He made a joke about losing the election. The jury did not laugh.

He testified that Carl had a good reputation as a lawyer. On cross-examination, when asked about Carl's actions, Judge Wilson endorsed Carl's defense, Grace's signed a release, she was an adult.

During closing arguments, Carl's lawyer, Sid Thurlow, took the jury on a tour of Carl's defense. By happenstance, the trash can next to the court reporter was overflowing with papers and partially filled coffee cups. Sid was standing in front of the trash can. As he talked, he would back up, ever so slightly. The trash can would tip ever so slightly. Sid had no clue what was happening behind him, but the jury did. They were fascinated, paying rapt attention to the ever-tipping coffee-filled trash can. By now, the jury was paying little attention to Sid, who finally succeeded in knocking the entire mess across the courtroom carpet. His rhythm was broken. So was his argument.

The jury returned Grace's property and, to punish Carl, awarded her additional punitive damages of $100,000. But Carl was not through.

He appealed the case. Once the judgment was thirty days old, we could send it to the sheriff to foreclose on Carl's property and bank accounts to collect the $100,000. The only way for Carl to prevent this was to post a bond to guarantee the payment of the money. If he lost on appeal, we were guaranteed to collect Grace's money. To our great and grateful surprise, he posted the $100,000 bond.

The three appellant judges denied Carl's appeal, writing, "Baker engaged in an unbelievable course of conduct," reciting Carl's misdeeds proven at trial.

Two years later, I picked up the phone and a man asked, "What do you know about Carl Baker?"

I answered, "A lot. Why do you want to know?"

This man relayed that his seventy-five-year-old widowed mother had hired Carl to represent her in a matter a few years back. Carl concluded the case and, in doing so, became her confidant, coming to her house and showering her with attention—enough attention to convince her to loan him $200,000. Looking at the dates, it became apparent where Carl got the money to post the appeal bond.

Dolefully, I told the man that Carl was bankrupt. There was little chance to recover the money. The only solace I could give him and his mother—Carl was disbarred.

22

Kidnapping in the Middle East

"YOU'RE A FIVE-YEAR-OLD GIRL. YOUR PARENTS ARE separated. You live with your mother most of the time. You have your room and your toys and your friends. Your father, who speaks English and another language, picks you up on weekends and other days for you to stay with him. Then he brings you back to Mommy. One day, Daddy picks you up and takes you to the airport, where the two of you get on a plane. You are on the plane for so long that you fall asleep. When you awaken and disembark, you're in unfamiliar surroundings. The people speak a different language, and the streets and buildings don't look like home.

"You ask Daddy, 'When can I go home to Mommy?'

"He says, 'This is your new home. Mommy's not here.' He takes you to his parents' house in Damascus, Syria, where your grandmother greets you in Daddy's language. She shows you to 'your room.' You are sad, lonely, and scared." (From the Introduction to The International Child Abduction Act.)

This scenario has become increasingly more common as easy travel and educational opportunities for foreigners coming to America result in more and more marriages across various geographic boundaries.

Typically, if a child is abducted to a foreign country, there are treaties to facilitate their return. But no treaties or remedies exist in the Middle East under Islamic law.

If the mother of an abducted child goes to such a country for assistance, the authorities and court system will refuse to help her. The father has absolute control over his wife and children. If she goes to the US embassy in that country, she will be told that there is nothing they can do to help. "We are in their country, and we are governed by their laws."

Theresa came into my office. She'd married a Syrian, Abdel, and they were headed for a divorce. Theresa feared he would take their five-year-old daughter, Susan, and infant daughter, Linda, to Syria. She had good reason for this fear. Just before Linda was born, he'd threatened to do that with Susan. And she had him on tape.

In one of their many arguments, Theresa told Abdel that she gave Susan's passport to her parents to ensure the child could not be taken out of the United States. Abdel responded, "I've got my ducks in a row. If you think you took precautions, I can have Susan travel on a Syrian passport." Like citizens from many Middle Eastern countries, Abdel had dual citizenship and could travel on his US or Syrian passport. His children were also dual citizens. Likewise, he could get Syrian passports for them.

Upon our filing for her divorce, the court noted we were asking for Theresa to have sole custody and to limit Abdel's visitation to the SAFE program, designed for at-risk parents to see their children. These visits are conducted in a pleasant environment supervised by Children's Protective Services. A plainclothes sheriff's deputy is always present. The visiting parent is never alone with the children nor allowed to remove them from SAFE.

At the preliminary hearing, the judge granted my request and entered two other orders. One appointed Dr. Jim Cox, a psychologist, to do a custody evaluation; the other appointed Sandra Palmer, an attorney, to represent the children.

Cox, as an evaluator, was charged with meeting with the parents and children, conducting psychological testing, reviewing pertinent documents, and interviewing individuals familiar with the family. The psychologist would then recommend to the judge which parent should have primary custody.

Having known Dr. Cox for years and having experience with him as an evaluator on other cases, I told Theresa that I could write his report before he even saw anyone. Cox was notorious, in my opinion, for his pedestrian work. His reports contained pages outlining his testing and work. No matter the facts, he would customarily opine, "I recommend that the parents be appointed joint conservators with the mother having primary possession of the children and the father being given liberal visitation."

Many cases require expert witnesses to help educate the court on matters unfamiliar to judges and laypeople. We chose Leigh Windsor as our expert witness on international abduction to Muslim countries.

Several years before, Leigh's children had been kidnapped to Syria by her Syrian husband. Having learned about Islamic law and the difficulties in child recovery from Muslim countries, she arranged clandestinely to recover her children. She later successfully organized the rescue from the Middle East of twenty abducted children. Using her background in psychology, she devised factors to profile a potential Middle Eastern abductor and published a book about her experiences and findings.

She had also worked with the State Department, the Justice Department, the United Nations, and Congress on international child abduction cases. She had provided technical support to the FBI and Interpol to create strategies for the return of abducted children. She was an incredible expert witness. Her signs of a potential abductor were later turned into law by the Texas Legislature.

In this case, she testified that Abdel fit the profile of a potential abductor, and he was a risk to kidnap the children based on the following evidence and testimony:

Threats are a major indication of the potential for abduction. We had Abdel's "I've got my ducks in a row" tape.

Theresa testified that he had threatened to take the children to Syria to be raised by his mother, sister, or new wife, where she would never see them again. He denied these statements.

Testimony was introduced that Susan said, "Daddy said I can become a fairy and fly away," indicating that she would not see her mother again.

Abdel's response: "Kids make stuff up."

Abdel had written a will in Arabic one year before, giving his mother in Syria guardianship of the children and leaving all of his assets to her.

His sister, who was living overseas, came to testify on his behalf. On cross-examination, she stated that the name on her passport was Mohamed, the same as Abdel's. When pressed, she admitted she could pass as the children's mother on an international flight.

Other than his job, Abdel had no ties to the United States. He had previously worked in Syria and traveled to China, Indonesia, the United Arab Emirates, France, Jordan, Bahrain, and Saudi Arabia.

Abdel testified that he considered his immediate family to be his parents and sisters, who lived in Syria. Only when prompted by his lawyer did he include his wife and children as his family.

Theresa testified that Abdel had boasted to her that he was a member of the Muslim Brotherhood and had shown her a picture of him in army fatigues, holding a rifle. He said her testimony was false.

We learned that Abdel's mother's cousins worked at the US embassy in Damascus, and he had an uncle who held a security position at the Damascus airport—another daunting obstacle to any attempt from Theresa to retrieve her children from Syria.

Dr. Cox's report contained copious pages regarding his work, along with his customary hefty bill. As expected, Dr. Cox recommended that Judge Dempsey name the parents as joint custodians, with Theresa having primary possession, and that Abdel enjoy liberal visitation. No provisions were addressed in his report about parental kidnapping concerns, though Theresa had forcefully expressed them to Cox.

Abdel's lawyer, Joan Ayres, was the first to question Cox. She began by addressing the topic hovering over the courtroom. "Are you aware of the allegations made by Theresa regarding her fears that Abdel will take the children to Syria?"

He replied, "Very much so."

"Based on your investigation and professional training, do you believe her concern is valid?"

"No," Cox said.

After more questioning, it was my turn.

"Do you agree that your conclusions and recommendations are just your personal opinions?"

Cox replied, "They are based on my professional training and observations."

Cox had deflected the question. I objected, and Judge Dempsey ordered him to answer whether or not his report was just his personal opinion.

Cox reluctantly agreed.

In a series of questions, he agreed that:

1. He was not an expert on the Middle East.
2. He was not an expert on the Muslim religion.
3. He was not an expert on Islamic law.
4. He was not an expert on profiling abductors.
5. He was not an expert on preventing abductions to the Middle East.

Going further, I pressed, "Dr. Cox, if the children were kidnapped to the Middle East and prevented from seeing their mother again, would they suffer irreparable harm?"

Cox had to agree.

"Do you agree that if a mother fears her child will be abducted, she should take steps to prevent it?"

Again, he had to agree.

Throughout the trial, Sandra, the court-appointed children's lawyer, asked very few questions helpful to our case, but appeared sympathetic to testimony helpful to Abdel. I thought she was failing as an advocate for the children. I was always friendly with Sandra, and we got along professionally, but I could not resist. Turning to her at the counsel table, I asked, "Are you hearing the same testimony I am?" She just raised her eyebrows.

Mary Thompson was Abdel's expert witness. She represented herself as an expert on international abductions, having some of the same experiences as Leigh, though her resume was much thinner. Because she was from Canada, I was reminded of the old lawyer adage, "Anyone from more than sixty miles out of town is an expert."

She prepared a report considering all factors, much the same as Leigh, but in her direct examination, she opined that Abdel was not a risk for the abduction of his daughters—a direct contradiction of what Leigh had told the court.

Leigh obtained a report that Thompson had provided in a Montreal custody case. Testifying for the mother in Canada, with facts and allegations eerily identical to our case, Thompson's opinion in Canada was that "The father posed a serious threat to abduct"—the exact opposite of the opinion she rendered in our case. I began my cross-examination by having her identify her Canadian report.

After comparing her two reports with their similar facts and starkly opposite conclusions, I asked, "Ms. Thompson, you would agree with me that the factors in your Canadian case are almost identical to the factors in this case?" She agreed they were "similar." I concluded, "Yet your conclusions as to the fathers' flight risks are totally opposite?" Again, she agreed … and I passed the witness. Joan took her back on redirect. Though Joan did her best, there was no way to rehabilitate this witness.

I opened the final argument by recounting the testimony and numerous contradictions Judge Dempsey had heard. Joan gave her closing, pointing out our extreme request that Abdel would never have standard visitation like other divorced fathers. She reminded the court of Cox's recommendations, the judge's selected evaluator.

Sandra's closing did not surprise me. She talked in general about the importance of children having a good relationship with both parents and the importance of coparenting. She opposed our request asking for supervised visitation in the SAFE program.

In closing, my final words to Judge Dempsey were, "For the last year, I've carried on my shoulders the burden of representing Theresa and protecting her children." I looked the judge in the eye and said, "I now pass that burden to you." The judge ever so slightly flinched. I happened to look at the bailiff. His reaction was a brief nod of his head and a slight smile at me.

Judge Dempsey took the case under advisement, meaning she wanted some time to fashion her decision.

We returned a few days later to hear the final orders. Theresa was given sole custody of the girls. Abdel's visitation would be limited to the SAFE program, and Theresa did not have to disclose her or the children's whereabouts to him.

After a victory in court, I am usually delighted. Though pleased with this result, I felt no joy. Sadly, these children would grow up without having two loving parents to share their lives. They would, however, grow up with a lot of questions. As they grew older, they could blame their mother for their lack of contact with their father. Years later, I learned that as adults, the girls' relationship with their mother was almost nonexistent, blaming her for growing up without their father. But they had reunited with Abdel. In hindsight, a predictable, unfortunate outcome.

But what if Abdel had picked them up for a visit, got on a plane, and they woke up in a foreign country—without Mommy?

23

The Most Famous Name in Football

WHEN I ANSWERED THE PHONE, THE VOICE was frail, but the clipped speech still dropped consonants. Like Jan Reid described him in *Texas Monthly* magazine, football was "fooball," business was "biness." Of course it was Jerry Argovitz. This was May 2024.

A dentist by training, he became a sports agent and legend, forcing NFL teams to pay athletes like Heisman Trophy winners Billy Sims and Herschel Walker more money than they had ever imagined. He was a nemesis to the NFL teams' owners. CBS sportscaster Brent Musberger said, "The most famous name in football today is Jerry Argovitz. He's not even a player, he's an agent."

It was Billy Sims who said, "Dr. Argovitz is the dentist who drilled the NFL for money and changed the way the game was played." Gene Klein, former owner of the San Diego Chargers, said, "Jerry Argovitz is a scumbag."

There was even talk from Hollywood about a movie based on his life.

A millionaire many times over, Jerry was also a land developer, founder of the United States Football League, owner of the Houston Gamblers, and a partner in three Native American casinos. And he was one of the most honorable men and smartest clients I ever had, and a friend for some forty years.

On the phone call, he said he wanted to see me. "Jerry, I retired five years ago. I don't even have an office," I responded.

"I don't care," he replied, "I need to see you."

As I arrived at his condominium overlooking the Houston skyline, his daughter Kari led me to the television room. Jerry, sitting in his chair, looked every one of his eighty-five years. But it was no surprise that his handshake was as firm as the first time I met him in 1982.

We enjoyed a common background. He grew up in the Panhandle town of Borger, some 200 miles from my hometown of Lamesa. Texans from that part of the state, born in the '30s and '40s, had much in common: flat plains, small towns, droughts, and beauty parlors and churches seemingly on every corner.

Jerry's family was different than others in Borger: They were the only Jewish family. When farming and ranching communities popped up in rural West Texas, it was common that a Jewish family would arrive to open a dry goods store, a general merchandise store, or—as with Jerry's family—a hardware store.

I recall our first meeting. He needed a divorce. He was exceedingly charming and all business.

Male divorce clients usually search for every avenue to minimize their financial loss. They view their assets as "my money." Jerry's first comment was different. "Tom, Elaine is the mother of my children. I want to take care of her."

Because it was our first meeting, I was skeptical of this comment coming from a man who was getting divorced. My skepticism was misplaced.

We discussed his marital estate as well as his children, their ages, schools, and facts about their young lives. He told me they were adopted.

Growing up in the Panhandle, he became a semi-professional boxer in order to earn money. He was a good one, at that. On Saturday nights, he would go to Amarillo to fight. The prize money was good. Like everything else he did in his later life, he excelled at boxing. In one fight, his opponent struck a low blow. The resulting condition meant he could never father a child.

I asked him why he became a boxer. His response, "Tom, you try to be the only Jew boy in Borger, Texas."

In an unusual twist of events, Elaine hired a Dallas lawyer, Edwin Sigel, to represent her. There were plenty of good divorce lawyers in Houston. In the numerous family law matters I have been involved in, this is the only one in which I recall a client hiring an out-of-town lawyer for a Houston case. She paid Edwin a retainer of $10,000—a generous amount in 1981. Rather than come to Houston, Sigel hired a local lawyer, Bernard Hebinik, to do the actual work.

Bernie was a competent lawyer. I had several cases against him in the past and we were collegial with each other.

In most cases of divorce, the first thing that occurs is the entry of temporary orders. These orders are designed to maintain the status quo while the case is pending. Both parties are prohibited from hiding and wasting assets or harming or harassing each other, among other things. Orders are also entered regarding possession of houses, children, child support, and temporary alimony. Most of the time, lawyers and clients agree on these matters without the necessity of going to court. We agreed on all issues—except money.

The family district court judges hire associate judges. One of their jobs is to hear contested motions for temporary orders. If one of the parties does not agree with the associate judge's ruling, they can appeal to the district judge.

Associate Judge Volley Bastine heard our case. At the conclusion, he ordered Jerry to pay Elaine $1,000 per month in child support and $5,000 per month in alimony—a significant award in 1981 dollars.

Elaine hired Earle Lilly to replace Bernie and Sigel. Earle immediately appealed Judge Bastine's decision.

To call Earle flamboyant and tough is an injustice to those words. Earle would go to extreme lengths for his clients. It was rumored that in a custody case representing the father, Earle had cocaine planted in the mother's car, then the police received an anonymous call. He counted on opposing parties being intimidated by his reputation—but Jerry was not.

By coincidence, the hearing on the appeal of Judge Bastine's order was scheduled during the week the Aloha Bowl was being played in Honolulu. This game pitted the best college football players in the country against one another. The NFL teams wanted to recruit them, and you could bet that the better players needed Jerry to represent them.

Jerry called. He had to be in Hawaii. By then, he was the most famous sports agent in the country. These were players he could recruit. Not only would they make a lot of money, but so would Jerry. In our motion, we reminded the court that Jerry's success would also benefit Elaine.

The hearing was postponed. Upon Jerry's return, Judge Peavy, the district judge, heard the appeal and affirmed Judge Bastine's earlier ruling.

Lawyers in divorce cases make every effort to determine the parties' assets, values, and debts. In a case involving millions of dollars, this requires the production of thousands of pages of documents. We didn't wait for Earle to make a formal "discovery" request. I knew what he needed. I provided Jerry with a comprehensive list of documents to give to Earle. If Earle needed something else, we immediately sent it to his office.

It took Earle months to review this mountain of material. Once he did, negotiations for a final settlement started.

This was one time this man who intimidated NFL team owners put away his sword. Good to his word from the first time I met him, he made Elaine a generous offer, which she accepted.

Many years later, when I saw Jerry on that day in May, one of the first things he said to me was, "Elaine and I are still good friends." It proved that he lived by his three rules. Rule 1: Do the Right Thing. Rule 2: Always do the right thing. Rule 3: If you forget what to do, go back to Rules 1 and 2.

These rules also guided his representation of professional athletes. He affectionately called them "my sons." He negotiated millions of dollars for them while also providing them with financial advisers. This would guarantee that they could enjoy a lifetime of financial comfort when their playing careers ended.

Jerry once told me, "Tom, most of these young Black players were raised without a father. It was their mother or grandmother who took care of them. Every time I negotiate the money that a team will pay them, the first thing they do is take care of the women who raised them."

Once I was working in one of Jerry's offices when a young Black football player whose name I never learned came in. "Mister, do you mind if I use your phone?" He then dialed a number. Barely containing his emotion, he said that he had signed with an NFL team and exclaimed, "Mama, Mama. I'm gonna get two million dollars! Mama, I'm gonna build you a house! I'm gonna build you a house!"

It was late Fall 2003 when Jerry came to my office to reveal to me that his fifteen-year marriage to Paddy Argovitz had come to an end. She had filed for divorce, and he wanted my help. Before this case was over, it would go to the Court of Appeals.

Jerry described Paddy as a beauty. She had been Mrs. America in 1981. When I met her, I could see where she had once been a blonde beauty. Now plastic surgery and Botox had rendered her face immobile.

The marital estate was complex, with numerous limited partnerships and ventures. Again, we produced thousands of pages of documents and appraisals to Paddy's lawyers and accountants. After many months, her lawyers were satisfied that they had all the information they needed to proceed to a settlement.

After multiple mediation conferences with Randy Wilhite, one of the best divorce mediators in Texas, Jerry and Paddy entered into a binding agreement as to the division of their assets. We drafted the necessary closing documents to finalize the divorce and sent them to Paddy's attorneys. Paddy refused to approve the settlement.

Because of her refusal, we were required to draft a final decree of divorce incorporating the agreement and ask the court to enter it without Paddy's or her lawyer's approval. Paddy took the position that our documents did not reflect the terms of their deal. The judge ordered us to return to Randy, who now became an arbitrator to judge drafting disputes. After Randy made some minor changes, the judge entered our decree over Paddy's objections.

The deal was complicated. The properties divided took up more than fourteen pages of the final order, single spaced.

In the many hours we spent drafting the documents, Jerry was with us every step of the way. My long-time paralegal Angie Byrnes commented, "Jerry is the smartest client we've ever had."

I agreed. His attention to detail was incredible. His editing and revising of the paperwork showed us why he was so successful in everything he touched. I jokingly told him that I should hire him as a second paralegal.

Paddy and Jerry had twelve assets that could not be easily divided. This required Jerry to continue to manage them until such time as the investments were liquidated or finalized. This included three casinos.

Paddy and Jerry spent much of their married life in Las Vegas. During that time, Jerry became friends with Kevin Kean, who was noted for assisting Native Americans to achieve economic independence. One way he did this was by negotiating tribal gaming compacts with state and federal officials. These agreements allowed tribes to operate casinos. And the tribes needed outside investors to make the casinos a reality. Jerry and Kean developed three casino ventures with tribes in Michigan and California.

For Jerry to manage these complex assets, each party was required to put $25,000 in a management account for Jerry to pay expenses. If the account fell below the sum of $20,000, each party had to contribute an additional $10,000. If either one failed to do this, then that party would forfeit all interest in these assets, which were worth millions of dollars.

The account fell below $20,000. Jerry put up his $10,000. He demanded Paddy put up her share. She refused. He gave her a second demand, giving her an additional ten days to pay. She refused again.

Paddy then sued Jerry, saying he had mismanaged the assets and demanded an accounting. And now, five months too late after his request for $10,000, Jerry received a check from Paddy for $20,000. I returned her check to her lawyer, along with my motion declaring that she had forfeited her interests in these valuable properties.

As to Paddy's claim of mismanagement, Jerry opened all books to her accounting expert, Bill Stewart. Bill was not only a CPA but also a certified fraud examiner. He testified at a hearing that Jerry had shown him all the records he needed to see and was very forthcoming, but he criticized some of Jerry's accounting practices.

Paddy's counsel's examination of Jerry was even more enlightening.

Lawyer: "You're aware of numerous requests for accounting regarding monies received and expenses paid?"

Jerry: "I'm aware of letters you have written requesting such things. Your mischaracterization and misunderstanding of the divorce decree is obvious."

The court ruled. Jerry had done nothing wrong. Then the judge ruled that Paddy had forfeited her entire interest in these valuable assets. One hundred percent of these assets were now Jerry's property. Her loss was staggering.

Paddy's next step was the Court of Appeals. She contended that the divorce decree did not require her to make the cash call as Jerry's request was improper and again claimed that he had mismanaged the assets, so the resulting ruling that she had forfeited her assets was wrong. In a thirty-four-page opinion, the Court of Appeals rejected her claims except one, which was a minor victory for her. For a second time, a court ruled he was now the owner of one hundred percent of these properties.

Years later, Judge Frank Rynd, who presided over the divorce and ruled on Paddy's forfeiture, told me that this was one of the most difficult decisions he ever made—he knew what it would cost her.

That May day in 2024 would be the last time I would see Jerry. As I reached over and hugged Jerry, he said, "Tom, I love you." It was easy for me to say, "I love you, Jerry."

He died of pancreatic cancer three days later.

24

More Tales

WHEN A RETIRED LAWYER STARTS RECOUNTING STORIES from his personal and professional life, he tries to categorize people, events, and fascinating bits of information. My writing experience soon prompted me to wonder what I should do with tales that don't quite make up a chapter but certainly are seared in my memory.

Knowing that a writer of a memoir can't remember everyone and everything, I—like many others—have tried to recall many of these lifetime highlights. So here are some short stories that were interesting or fun to recall.

Dr. Denton Cooley

Denton Cooley was a world-famous heart surgeon in Houston who implanted the first artificial heart in a human being.

Willie Walker, also a heart surgeon, was married to Mary Cooley, Dr. Cooley's youngest daughter. Knowing a divorce was imminent, Willie hired me to represent him.

The most contentious aspect of the divorce was the ownership of the Walker family home. The large River Oaks house was next door to Dr. and Mrs. Cooley. Mary claimed it was her separate property, a gift from her parents, who had paid for the house.

Dr. Cooley's deposition was scheduled, and I asked Mary's attorney to provide me with his tax returns. Understanding that tax returns are privileged information, I had no right to see them. To my amazement, her attorney requested Dr. Cooley to provide his returns, and he did.

My reason for seeing the returns was to verify a hunch. Dr. Cooley could afford the best accountants in Houston. My guess was that they advised him to take a gift tax exemption for both Mary and Willie on the River Oaks house. If that was the case, the house was not a gift to Mary, but a joint gift to both Mary and Willie.

The day of the deposition came. I knew Dr. and Mrs. Cooley, having met them several times on social occasions. Though we did not know each other well, he knew that we'd had prior introductions. Starting the deposition, I reminded him that he was under oath and ensured that he understood the necessity of providing accurate answers.

With the preliminaries aside, I went straight to the heart of the matter. "Dr. Cooley, you are a world-famous surgeon, but you are not a CPA?" I asked.

"Correct," he answered.

Handing him one of his returns, I asked, "I know you are not an accountant, but if you're like me, you review these returns before you sign?"

"Yes."

"Because you want to see if there are any glaring mistakes that you could correct?" I hedged.

"Yes."

"And you understand that when you sign a return, it is under the pains and penalties of perjury."

"Yes."

"Please turn to Form 709. Do you recognize that as the form where you report gifts?" I asked.

I could see Dr. Cooley tensing. He seemed to have sensed something unpleasant was coming. He answered that he recognized the form.

The returns showed just what I predicted. I continued, "And you are swearing to the IRS that you made gifts regarding the Del Monte home to Willie and Mary?"

Dr. Cooley, knowing the ax had fallen, said, "Yes."

"And in so swearing, you made the gift not just to Mary, but to Willie as well?"

Dr. Cooley, glaring at me, replied, "Yes."

"And we have your last five years of returns here. If I go through each return, we will find that you were consistent in reporting these gifts to Willie and Mary?"

"Yes." Now he was coldly staring at me. He made an under-the-breath comment; though I could not hear it, I knew it was not a compliment. The entire room knew as well.

Having maintained a courteous demeanor with him throughout the deposition, I concluded, "Dr. Cooley, thank you for your patience and time today. Pass the witness." Mary's attorney had no questions.

The deposition was over. I packed my briefcase and started to leave as Dr. Cooley came to me and said, "Tom, can I have a minute with you?"

I stopped. And he continued, "I want to apologize to you for my behavior just now. That was uncalled for."

"Dr. Cooley," I replied, "no apology is needed. Blood is thicker than water. I understand."

Denton Cooley was a class act. We settled the case the following week.

Judge Peter Solito

Pete Solito was one of the finest and most respected judges in Texas.

Texas district courts have the broadest jurisdiction of any of the trial courts—greater than the county, probate, and justice of the peace courts. Judge Solito started his judicial career as a family law district court judge, then later a criminal district judge, then a civil district judge, ultimately becoming the chief judge of the sixty-seven Harris County district courts.

As a young lawyer trying one of my first jury cases, I made an objection. Judge Solito sustained, but I kept arguing my objection. He looked over his glasses at me and said, "Counselor, when the court agrees with you, it's time to sit down." A couple of jurors chuckled.

Lesson learned.

In 1986, I was elected to the board of directors for the State Bar of Texas. All lawyers in Texas must be members of the state bar, and the board is its governing body. It was an honor to be elected to a three-year term. Judge Solito was chosen to be the judicial liaison to the board for the same term as mine.

Bar boards become a cohesive group of friends. Though we may have had policy differences, we made great friendships. Meetings were held four times a year over a period of several days. We would meet around the state, taking our spouses and significant others with us. At night, we would have dinner together or be treated to special events. We became great friends with lawyers and significant others from across Texas.

Pete and his wife, Sallie, lived close to us. As couples, we got in the habit of traveling together to the meetings. We became especially close, going to their house on many occasions. Many nights, we would be there along with other attorneys and judges. Pete was admired and loved by many.

At the conclusion of one board meeting in El Paso, Pete, Sallie, Anne, and I went to the airport to catch our flight home to Houston. The wives had already entered the terminal. Pete and I were standing in line with our luggage to give to the skycap.

As we inched to the front of the line, there was a man ahead of us loudly berating the skycap about some insignificant matter.

Then it was our turn. Ever calm, Pete said to the skycap, "That fellow wasn't very nice to you."

The skycap replied, "No sir, he wasn't. Too bad. He's going to Dallas. But his bags are going to Chicago."

Pete and I vowed always to be kind to skycaps and to tip generously.

Pete died several years later. I was honored to be one of his pallbearers with, among others, my friend Joe Jamail.

Pete was a great judge and a great friend. I still miss him.

How Marla Maples Met Donald Trump

While visiting with Jerry Argovitz one afternoon, he recounted an event in his relationship with Donald Trump.

Trump owned the New Jersey Generals, and Jerry owned the Houston Gamblers, both teams in the nascent United States Football League. Trump would later cause the death of the USFL, trying to cut an under-the-table deal with the NFL to acquire a team in the New York area.

While Jerry and Trump were still on good terms, Jerry was invited to judge a beauty contest in Florida. The runner-up was Marla Maples.

Marla knew that Trump and Jerry were acquaintances through the USFL, and Marla wanted to meet Trump. She asked Jerry to provide an introduction. Jerry agreed, but before he did so, he turned to Marla and said, "Be sure and hire a good lawyer."

Cows and Horses

A clever fellow once remarked, "Guys raised in small towns can't wait to get away. They go to the city, make some money, and then want to return to the country life."

That was me.

In 1995, Anne and I bought acreage near Round Top, Texas, where I could keep horses and start a small "cow-calf" operation. Many city folks who acquire a piece of country property will erect a gate with a sign atop, giving it a grand name like "El Rancho de Los Caballeros" or some such. Their next acquisition will be a longhorn steer, what I call "pasture eye-candy."

Having grown up in West Texas, I knew ranches consisted of sections of land, 640 acres per section. I knew I would be asked, "What are you naming your ranch?" My response, with a smile, was, "There's a mailbox. It says 'Conner' in inch-high letters." I call it "my farm." And no, I did not buy a longhorn steer.

I'll be the first to admit that over those years, I owned a lot of four-legged creatures who could eat while I was asleep, and I never made a profit. But there was immeasurable pleasure, returning to my Texas roots.

And I had some good horses over my lifetime. Churchill is credited with saying, "There's nothing better for the inside of a man than the outside of a horse."

Riding for pleasure for most of my life, I can say that yes, their outside always made my inside feel good.

People who aren't familiar with horses may be unaware that they can bond with their owners much like a faithful dog. And over the years, I have had many faithful dogs and horses. A wish of mine: If there is an afterlife, I hope all my dogs and horses are there to greet me.

The Bull Fight

One Saturday afternoon during the El Paso State Bar board meeting, the director from that border city arranged a trip for the members and spouses to Juárez to watch some young wannabe matadors spar with some young bulls.

These bulls were maybe a year and a half old. The announcer asked if any of us wanted to try our hand. Several of the directors, knowing I spent a lot of time with horses and cattle, urged me to get in the small arena.

Having seen bullfights before and having read *Death in the Afternoon* and *The Sun Also Rises*, I had a good idea that the bull's attention would be on the cape, not me. So I agreed.

As I held my cape, a young bull, his inexperience equal to mine, was released from the chute. He looked quizzically at me. I shook the cape. He ran toward me. I put the cape close to the ground. He lowered his head and charged.

Swirling the cape around me, the young bull's horns followed the cape. It felt good. After a few more times, my heart said, "Do it again." My head said, "Don't push your luck."

With a little bravado, I turned my back on the bull, as I had seen matadors do, and walked to the stands to a rousing ovation.

The Sand Blows

When I was five years old, the drought in West Texas and I were the same age. Much like in the Dust Bowl of the '30s, the wind would pick up, and the dry, red sand would blow and blow.

There was a big "blow" coming. We were living in the country at that time. Dad came and picked Mom and me up to take us to town to stay in a motel until the sandstorm subsided.

We returned to the farm after spending three days in the motel. Dad had to hire a road grader to clear the road to the house, as sand had drifted over it, much like a snowstorm. Of course, the interior of the house was covered with dirt, and it was a monumental effort to clean it.

As Mom said to my Grandmother Ruby, who came to Texas from Alabama in 1893, "Mother, you think you were a pioneer. Well, you never lived through anything like a West Texas sandstorm."

He Got to Ride Downtown

Recalling Professor Hippard's advice about dealing with police, "You may beat the rap, but you can't beat the ride downtown." Someone didn't listen.

Some three weeks went by after the professor's advice. Dan Dugan, a classmate, was at a bar on Saturday night. He was overserved and the bouncer told him to leave. Dugan began to explain to the bouncer in an argumentative voice, "I'm in law school and I know my rights."

The law school comment was the perfect invitation for an off-duty cop.

A patrol car arrived; Dan enjoyed a ride in the back seat and a night in the city jail. He called Professor Hippard, who, getting him released the next morning, commented, "You might pay better attention in my class."

Call the Pilot

Over the years, I've represented several oil men in Midland, Texas, the heart of the Permian Basin, 86,000 square miles of oil rich real estate.

These men amazed me. They had ice water in their veins and were sinking holes in the ground even when oil prices were sinking too. They also lived the high life.

I was on the phone with one of my clients, Bill Evans, who had leases throughout the Permian Basin and was drilling wells as fast as he could. During the phone call, he asked, "Who are the Rangers playing tonight?" He was referring to the baseball team, the Texas Rangers.

Me: "I have no clue."

Him: "I'm talking to my secretary." She responded it was the Yankees.

Him, to her: "Call the pilot. Tell him we're going to the game tonight."

This Was Fun

When we sold the Round Top farm, my family thought I would get in a blue funk, missing it. That piece of Texas dirt certainly had brought a lot of pleasure to me.

It was a couple of weeks before the sale was to be finalized. That winter day brought blowing rain and forty degrees on the thermometer. I was atop a tractor, putting round bales of hay out. The wet and hungry cattle were excitingly mooing when they saw me coming.

On the ground, cutting the baling strings so I could drop the hay into the feed ring, my 2,000-pound bull was no help. He pushed and ate on the winter forage. He did a fair job of almost knocking me over. Whacks with an old fence post on his hard head had no effect.

Completing my task, cold and wet, I closed the gate and remounted the tractor. Heading for the barn, I thought, "I remember when this was fun."

Dr. P

Dr. Richard Paul was one of the most noted psychiatrists in Texas. Having known him for years, I called him "Dr. P," and he called me for some legal advice.

He was retained in his professional capacity by Edwin Smith, a lawyer who represented a wealthy woman, Esther Graham. Well, she was wealthy until her husband convinced her to sign over her entire separate estate to him, as his separate property.

Edwin hired Dr. P to do a forensic examination of Esther Graham to determine if she had the mental capacity to be aware of the consequences of her generosity. After numerous sessions, he came to the opinion that she lacked the mental capacity to make informed decisions, especially at the time she'd handed over her property to her husband, Sam. Dr. P also opined that Sam had coerced her to the point that she was unable to resist his demands.

Dr. P reported his opinions to the court, making them an official court document.

Gary Estes was Sam's lawyer. He had been a partner in a major Houston law firm but left to specialize in family law as a solo practitioner. He had a reputation of being well-prepared and smart. Not this time.

He sent Dr. P a letter. "If you don't withdraw your opinion and state that she was mentally competent, I will sue you for slander and damages for falsifying your report." Dr. P showed me the letter. This had the definite aroma of subornation of perjury.

At a hearing a couple of weeks later, I had Estes on the witness stand. The examination was brief. He identified the letter and read the damning portion aloud.

Opening the Texas Criminal Code, I read, "subornation of perjury is a crime that involves persuading someone to commit perjury or lying under oath in a legal proceeding."

At that point, Judge Grace Hanson leaned over her bench. "I'm adjourning this proceeding to allow Mr. Estes to employ counsel. Mr. Estes, I advise you to engage a lawyer before you are asked to return to the witness stand."

To Dr. P's relief and enjoyment, I received a letter of retraction from Estes that afternoon.

The Chat and Chew

Jake Dobbins lived in Andrews, Texas, some thirty miles from Midland. He had a problem in probate court.

Jake's mother had died some years back, and his father, Fred, remarried. Fred passed away and the will left all his worldly assets to Jake, with appropriate provisions to care for his second wife. She was not satisfied. She contended the will only applied to the separate assets Fred owned and not to community assets. She wanted her half. Jake hired me to untangle the mess.

We engaged in the customary discovery, hiring of experts, and eventually going to mediation. We resolved the case to Jake's satisfaction.

The case wasn't particularly unusual, but Fred was.

Fred had a seventh-grade education. As a young teen, he went to work for his uncle, who owned the Chat and Chew Cafe in Andrews. In his early twenties, Fred bought that cafe.

Many of his customers were oil men: drillers, land men, equipment operators, the characters who inhabit the oil patch. Fred became friends with them, listening and learning about their business.

Fred figured out there was money to be made in the oil business other than by drilling. He focused on equipment: drilling rigs, workover rigs, valves, flanges, tanker trucks, and the myriad other things that make oil fields work.

The oil industry goes through booms and busts. It always has, and probably always will. During a bust, the price of idle oil field equipment craters to amazing lows.

The next bust came. Fred was ready. He had scraped some money together and started buying idle equipment at bargain prices. He patiently waited for the next boom. When it arrived, Fred sold his used equipment for a fat profit. He did that for almost three decades.

When Fred died in 2008, he was worth $25 million.

The Old Capitol Club

When I was a young lawyer, Texas did not sell liquor by the drink. To buy a cocktail in a bar required membership in a private club, so I joined the Old Capitol Club located in the historic Rice Hotel. It was the watering hole where the evenings found judges, legislators, and power brokers.

Presiding over the club's main table most nights was Everett Collier, the editor of the *Houston Chronicle*, the city's leading newspaper. He was a kingmaker. All through the '60s and into the late '70s, anyone aspiring to elected office in Harris County needed the *Chronicle*'s endorsement—that is, Everett Collier's endorsement.

It was amazing when judges walked in from the courthouse to hear Everett proclaiming, "Here come my boys." And some evenings, I would ingratiate myself by driving one of the overserved judges home.

Each table was graced with a large bowl of popcorn that the waiters replenished from large barrels in the storeroom. One night, a judge made a wrong turn to the men's room. He relieved himself in one of the barrels: the end of popcorn on the tables.

Another distinction about the OCC: All the waiters were ex-convicts. It was interesting to watch as they served judges who had sentenced them to prison.

And one night was a tad more distinct than most.

Anne and I were engaged. We were at the OCC and sitting at a table with Judge Solito and several others. After a few drinks, he decided he would go ahead and marry us. Having a large group stand up as witnesses, he proceeded to give us our vows, prompting our dutiful "I do's."

The Texas Family Code had been adopted earlier that year, providing the requirements for a legal marriage in Texas.

The next morning, Judge Solito called one of the authors of the law, Bob Dabney. He repeated the events of the prior evening with the comment, "My God, Dab. Tell me I didn't marry that couple." To his relief, Dab said, "No you didn't, Judge, but you might be more careful in the future."

Not One Word of English

When we bought the farm in Round Top, our neighbor was an old German, his grandparents having immigrated from the old country to Texas in the 1800s.

Ivan Cordes was a cowman all of his life. He could repair just about anything. Though approaching eighty, he could still drive his tractor and bulldozer. Ivan taught me a lot about cows, tractors, hay, repairs, and country common sense.

Ivan could be a curmudgeon. One example of this revolved around the Chicken Ranch, a bordello dating back to the early 1900's. The name came from the Depression era when chickens served as legal tender for the ladies' favors. The Chicken Ranch served as inspiration for the musical and movie The Best Little Whorehouse in Texas. Its location was only ten miles from us until it was shut down after an exposé by a Houston TV reporter. Ivan, like many locals in that area, hated Channel 13's Marvin Zindler. As far as the local citizens were concerned, the Chicken Ranch didn't bother anyone. Miss Edna, its proprietor, was a good citizen, supporting Boy Scouts, the county fair, and other community activities. She had strict rules for her "boarders," and they were never a nuisance or embarrassment to the locals. I soon learned not to mention Marvin Zindler to Ivan.

One day, he was railing about Mexicans coming to this country and not learning English. My Hispanic helper was extremely talented, hardworking, and trustworthy. It irked Ivan that Adan and I would speak Spanish and English to each other, him learning English and me improving my Spanish. Ivan could not understand why Adan was not already fluent in English. After one of his little fits about Mexicans and English, Ivan, with some pride, remarked, "You know, my grandmother came from

Germany, lived here thirty years, and never learned a word of English." The contradiction was inescapable. I held my tongue.

The High Country

The Weminuche Wilderness Area spans the Continental Divide. With a half-million acres, it is the largest wilderness area in Colorado, one of the federally designated lands for protection. The only way in or out is on horseback or foot and, pack your trash out. The goal: Leave nothing in the wilderness, except your footprints.

As a teenager and up through my late thirties, I was fortunate to spend several summers and falls taking pack trips in the Weminuche, riding up the Vallecito Creek or Pine River seeing deer, elk, bear, and beautiful mountain scenery. Along with our saddle horses, we had pack mules and horses carrying our supplies.

One vivid memory is arriving at an overlook. Down in the valley were two mirror image lakes, the Emeralds, their brilliant color giving them their name. At another overlook, we saw the historic mining town of Silverton, the slag heaps from the old silver mines still scarring the land. One summer, crossing the Continental Divide, while looking into Utah and New Mexico, snow fell on a July day.

One morning, we rode through a small ghost town named Tuckerville. The buildings had fallen down, but it was obvious this was once a small village. The legend is that a miner named Tucker discovered silver nearby. He was very careful when he went to town never to disclose the location of this valuable find. One day, as he was leaving town for his mine, two men followed him. Their tracking was successful. Tucker failed to realize he was being followed. The secret was soon out, others came to find their fortune, and the little town came to life. And, like most mines, the silver played out. The only vestiges remaining were the ruins we saw that morning and the sense of Mr. Tucker's lost dreams.

My local Colorado friends were elk hunters—not for trophies, but for winter food. A week before elk season, they rode up the Vallecito Creek into the wilderness to set up camp. I was fortunate to make this trek several times.

As for the campsite, they were seasoned pros, erecting a twenty-by-thirty-foot tent, with a sheepherder's stove inside to keep us warm. At night, it could be blowing snow. Inside, we were sitting in camp chairs, toasty in our long johns, the tent illuminated by Coleman lanterns.

One night, the tent flap was violently thrown open. A backpacker, his long hair and beard covered in icicles, looked inside and proclaimed, "Wow man. The Ritz!" Yes, we invited him to stay the night.

Not being an elk hunter, when 5 a.m. rolled around and my friends were up, climbing the mountains to work down the "chutes" looking for elk, I stayed in my bedroll. Awakening, after breakfast, I saddled my horse. In the gun scabbard, there was no rifle, but fly-fishing poles. I rode up to the high mountain lakes where the crystal-clear water presented one of nature's shows: large cutthroat trout lazily swimming.

And the night when the first elk was shot, we performed the rite of Native Americans by eating the liver. No, unlike our Native brothers, we did not eat it raw but prepared it as our mothers did: liver and onions in a cast-iron skillet.

Down in the valley at one of the local bars, the wives started joking that during hunting season, they should organize a "pleasure train." They could make a little money on the side with amorous visits to the hunting camps. Of course, it was just a joke.

On one elk trip, I took a friend from Houston. Sam had never been on anything like a pack trip. As we were riding up the switchbacks through fluffy white clouds, on impulse, I asked one of my friends, "Is the pleasure train coming this year?"

Don's response, "Yeah, they'll be in camp Wednesday."

It didn't take thirty seconds. My pilgrim friend asked, "What's the pleasure train?"

We knew the hook was set. Don commented over his shoulder, "They're some old mountain gals that make the camps. By Wednesday, they'll look pretty good."

Wednesday morning came, and I was saddling my horse, I told Sam to get his horse and let's fish the high lakes. "No, I'm going to stay in camp and read."

Our camp was some fifty yards off the main trail. As I rode in that evening, Sam was standing in the middle of that trail. Approaching, I could tell he had washed his hair and shaved. No small feat in the wilderness. I thought to myself, "This is priceless."

I asked, "Where are the girls?" It was obvious he was peeved when he reported they failed to appear. Of course, they never would.

Throughout the evening, there were complaints about our missing guests, Sam being the most vocal. We returned to Houston. Several months passed, and I saw Sam. Pointedly, he asked, "That pleasure train story. That was a dirty trick," but in much more colorful words.

I couldn't resist. "Yeah, you swallowed that hook pretty deep."

Alberto Pemex

In 1938, the president of Mexico sided with oil workers striking against foreign-owned oil companies for an increase in pay and social services. The now government-owned oil company was named Pemex. It is one of the largest oil companies in the world. When you pull into a gas station in Mexico, it carries the name Pemex.

When Anne was at the University of Texas, she and some other girls decided to spend the summer in Mexico City and study Spanish. The school they attended was locally known as the "Gringa University."

It was just a matter of days before the wealthy young Mexican boys were showing up in their European convertibles, courting the blonde Texas girls. The most inventive of this group introduced himself as Alberto Pemex, and Anne started dating him.

Alberto, whose real surname was Martinez, took her home one Sunday for a family dinner. His parents, siblings, and grandmother were at the table. Anne's Spanish was still in the learning phase. She knocked over a glass and announced, "*Estoy embarazada*," thinking she said, "I'm embarrassed." The only problem: What she actually said was, "I'm pregnant." The table had a good laugh, except for the grandmother. She never spoke to Anne again.

Cantinflas, Diego Rivera, and Gaia

Dev Moring is a fifth-generation resident of New Orleans, a fascinating man with a historic lineage including a former governor of Louisiana. His wife, Sally, and Anne were childhood friends in Houston. And the four of us became good couple friends.

During the early years of our marriage, we were their guests for Mardi Gras. Dev is a member of Momus, the second oldest "Krewe" in that annual pre-Lent celebration. Their float, parading through the streets of New Orleans is a favorite, known for its beauty and nationally famous guests. At the conclusion of the parade, their evening *bal masque* harkens back to the days of old New Orleans, reflecting the city's deep French roots. The members wear white ties and tails. The ladies are seated and the visiting gentlemen, like me, also in tails, are designated by the members to escort the ladies to the dance floor. And all are adorned with beautiful masks.

Dev's father owned a home in Cuernavaca, Mexico. When his dad passed away, Dev decided to sell the residence. He and Sally invited us for a weekend before the sale was concluded, during which, as always, they graciously entertained us.

Cuernavaca has long been a favorite escape for Mexico City residents and foreign visitors because of its warm, stable climate and abundant vegetation. Aztec emperors had summer residences there, as did Emperor Maxmillian I of Mexico, and the Shah of Iran lived there in exile. The Woolworth heiress and philanthropist Barbara Hutton, a friend of Dev's father, also had a home there.

We arrived one beautiful spring afternoon at the house, a block from the historic palace of the Spanish conquistador Hernán Cortés.

Upon entering the residence, our first sight was the open-air main room, furnished with beautiful antiques. From the balustrade, we gazed down on blooming hibiscus, lilies, and poinsettias. But among the lush gardens was the main attraction: A large swimming pool dominated in its center by a tile figure of the pre-Columbian goddess Gaia. Dev explained that the house once belonged to the celebrated Mexican comedian Cantinflas, who commissioned the design from the famed muralist Diego Rivera.

Some years later, we were visiting with another couple, whose son had recently married in Cuernavaca. In recounting their trip, they raved about a restaurant, extolling its charms. Their most vivid recollection was the view from their table, overlooking a pool with a tile figure designed by Diego Rivera. The restaurant's name: Gaia.

The Melodrama and Navajo Rugs

Durango is nestled in the San Juan Mountains in southwestern Colorado. This charming Old West town is historic for many reasons. It is the terminus of the Durango and Silverton Narrow Gauge Railroad, which takes passengers up the Animus River Valley to the historic mining town of Silverton. Its old steam locomotives still burn coal, and sometimes cinders get in the passengers' eyes, just like in the 1800s.

It is also famous for the Strater Hotel. Built in 1887, staying there takes the guests back in time to another era when the town was filled with miners searching for silver. Some guests claim they have seen ghosts at night in its old halls.

In the '60s and '70s, one Strater attraction was the Diamond Bell Theatre. Nightly melodramas were presented, just like in the frontier days. The audience booed and hissed at the villains and cheered the heroes. The actors were college drama students; the piano player wore spats and garters on his cuffs. It was authentic and fun.

One summer, I was hired to be the house manager, in charge of the ticket office, the bartenders, and the front of the house.

Jackson Clark was a regular patron. He was the Pepsi distributor in Durango. He often had guests in town, and he loved to take them to the Melodrama. He and I became friends, and when Jackson called, I moved reservations around to make sure he and his guests had front-row tables.

Jackson was a fourth-generation citizen of Durango. In the '40s, his parents would take Jackson and his sister on jaunts into the Navajo Reservation in western New Mexico and eastern Arizona. There were few roads, and these adventures stayed with Jackson. He became familiar with the terrain, the Navajo people, and the trading posts.

At the trading posts, the Navajos would get their supplies. Many times, they would bring their weavings and the turquoise jewelry they made to trade for their flour, beans, sugar, and necessities.

As a young man, Jackson worked for the original owner of the distributorship. One of the trading posts owed the Pepsi owner $1,000. He sent Jackson to collect.

On Jackson arriving at the trading post, the owner told him he had no money but offered to pay in Navajo rugs. Jackson took the rugs. Returning to the owner, with no money, but rugs, the owner was furious. But Jackson was confident. Within three weeks, he sold the rugs for $2,500, a nice $1,500 profit. The owner was pleased and Jackson continued to trade Pepsis for rugs throughout the time he owned the Pepsi plant.

As a result, Jackson became one of the most famous dealers in Navajo rugs in the Southwest. In his later years, he became friends with Mark Winter, the owner of the Toadlena Trading Post. To this day, it is still an authentic trading post on the reservation.

Jackson and Mark partnered and gathered a collection of rare Navajo weavings that they named the Durango Collection. They donated it to Fort Lewis College in Durango. If you are fortunate, you can visit this historic town and see this remarkable collection.

Henry Kissinger in the Land of Enchantment

In Santa Fe, I became friends with Don Lamm, the retired president of the New York publishing house W. W. Norton.

Over dinner one night, he recounted several stories. In one, he spoke of his friendship with Henry Kissinger, when Kissinger was a professor at Harvard. Norton was publishing his textbook on international relations, and he became an advisor to this storied publishing house.

During this time, Kissinger asked Don, "Where can I get away from people?" Don suggested Ruidoso, New Mexico. Kissinger spent a week one summer in this small ski resort and quarter-horse racing capital in southeastern New Mexico.

After Kissinger's return from Ruidoso, Don asked if he'd enjoyed it. He responded, "The only problem I had: I couldn't understand the people. They had a peculiar accent." What he did not realize was that most of the people inhabiting and visiting Ruidoso were from West Texas—towns like Lubbock, Plainview, Lamesa, Levelland, and the like. They all spoke with the pronounced West Texas twang.

Kissinger's next role would cement his fame: He became President Nixon's National Security Advisor.

Don then recounted that one of the largest challenges in book publishing was finding the right title. He had one book that he believed would be a bestseller, its working title: *A Short History of Practically Everybody.* Don suggested that the author, Jared Diamond, change it to *Guns, Germs, and Steel.* The book would sell in excess of 5 million copies.

The Little Prince

Ross Dinyari was a client and dear friend with a peculiar habit: Whenever he visited a city or area he liked, he would buy a house there. While this is an exaggeration, he did have some lovely homes in wonderful locations. One such house was in Quebec City in Canada.

One summer, Ross and his charming wife, Rosemarie, invited us to come and stay a few days. It was a glorious trip, and we were marvelously entertained. We seemingly had fresh foie gras each day, as the French farmers in the region were noted for this delicacy.

An interesting aspect of the trip was their home in the historic area of Quebec City. In 1942, the author Antoine de Saint-Exupéry and his wife stayed in Quebec, in the house now owned by the Dinyaris, and he began his famous book *The Little Prince*—a book that would sell over 140 million copies in 505 languages. The Quebec Historic Society placed a plaque on the exterior of the house extolling the significance of the residence.

Two years later, Anne and I were attending a meeting of the International Academy of Family Lawyers in Quebec, and we joined a guided group tour on a historic walk of this fabled and beautiful city.

We left the famous Frontenac Hotel and walked a short distance before turning onto a narrow street, which I immediately recognized as the location of the Dinyaris' house. The guide stopped and pointed out the plaque at 25 de la Rue Sainte-Genevieve, telling our group the story of Saint-Exupéry and *The Little Prince*. Anne and I smiled at each other. There was really no need to tell our group that we had enjoyed four nights in this lovely home.

Rancho Ancon

No longer a ranch, the old adobe house sits on four acres some 25 miles north of Santa Fe, New Mexico. Nestled in the valley of the Nambe River and surrounded by old cottonwoods, its interior is charming, containing classic Navajo weavings. In the entry is a rug woven around 1900 by the famous Navajo medicine man Hosteen Klah. The main room of the house was once part of the Pojoaque Pueblo and dates from the mid 1600's.

The Spaniards returned to New Mexico in 1703 following the Pueblo Revolt of 1680. One of the conquering Spaniards took possession of the pueblo structure and expanded the adobe house to four rooms.

Over the decades, Rancho Ancon was handed down to subsequent Spanish generations until 1930, when Chicagoan Eugene Van Cleeve acquired the ranch. He added guest bedrooms and opened a dude ranch. His wife, artist Elizabeth Boyd, was the founder of the Spanish Colonial Arts Museum in Santa Fe.

In 1943, Robert Oppenheimer was charged by President Roosevelt with developing the atomic bomb. In his search for a remote site to accomplish this top-secret task, Oppenheimer chose the small, isolated village of Los Alamos, located on a plateau 20 miles west of Rancho Ancon.

The roads to Los Alamos and Santa Fe were little more than packed dirt and gravel. Travel by car was slow and difficult. Having made his decision, Oppenheimer left Los Alamos for Santa Fe. Time was of the essence to report the Los Alamos location to Washington.

There were no phones in Los Alamos. He began his return to Santa Fe and inquired where a telephone could be found. The nearest was at Rancho Ancon. He arrived that winter afternoon, made the historic call, and spent the night. His assigned task was successful. The atomic bombs dropped on Japan in August 1945 ended World War II.

My connection to Rancho Ancon, although not historic, has provided me with pleasure over the years.

Gip Brown, my college roommate at the University of Texas, is still one of my closest friends. His great aunt, Agnes James, whom we called Aggie, acquired Rancho Ancon in 1949, after the majority of the acreage had been sold.

Aggie was famous in the early 1950s as a dress designer, having stores in Santa Fe and Albuquerque. In 1951, she was featured on the cover of *Women's Wear Daily*. She had no children; Gip was her nephew, but she treated him more like a grandson, and she adored him.

One Christmas break, Gip and I ventured to Rancho Ancon. Arriving at the snow-covered adobe, we found Aggie had young boys lighting *farolitos* across the roof. These small paper bags with candles stuck in sand at the bottom are a New Mexico Christmas tradition.

Getting out of the car, our first sensation was the aroma of piñon wood burning in the kiva fireplaces. I explored the house, finding the kitchen where Oppenheimer made that historic call. When I saw it for the first time in 1968, it had changed little since that 1943 winter afternoon.

The following summer, we returned. Sitting in the main room, we could hear Aggie on the phone in her small office. "My nephew and a friend are here. I've got some of your books I want to send as gifts. I'm sending the boys up with them for you to sign."

She came into the main room. "Boys, there's a stack of Georgia O'Keefe coffee table books by the door. Take them up to Georgia to sign." We were about to meet one the most famous artists of all time!

Excitedly, we jumped in our car and drove the thirty minutes to the small village of Abiqui, New Mexico. We arrived at Georgia's adobe house on a small mesa, now visited by hundreds of tourists each year. A small Mexican woman responded to our knock on the door. Silently, she took the books and shut the door. After waiting in the courtyard for some fifteen minutes, she reappeared, handing us the now autographed books. Gip and I "almost" met Georgia O'Keefe.

After college, Gip moved to Santa Fe, became a state government official, and lived at Rancho Ancon, caring for Aggie in her later years. He lives there to this day with his wife, Joanie.

In 2016, Anne and I bought a house in Santa Fe, and we have spent many delightful afternoons and evenings at Rancho Ancon. The kitchen has not changed since that first time I saw it in 1968, nor from what it looked like to Robert Oppenheimer on that winter day in 1943.

Will

Will Conner is one great guy. Of course, as his dad, what would you expect me to say?

Will is an Eagle Scout, like every man who's walked on the moon.

He is generous of his time and talent. In high school, he spent one summer in a small Mexican village with Amigos de las Americas. He and his companions taught the children basic hygiene and English. The villagers cooked on open fires. Will and his group taught them how to build clay ovens inside their houses, one step into modernization.

Fresh out of college, he worked for Texas Children's Hospital. Only he and the administrator had remote access to the hospital's website to inform the staff of emergencies, such as severe weather events, that would affect operations.

He left the hospital to perform marketing for a small startup coatings company that grew into Seal for Life, a subsidiary of Henkel, a large German company. He is the marketing manager for six brands, overseeing imaging for these companies that provide coating technologies for the petrochemical industry, shipbuilding, pulp and paper, commercial construction, renewable energy, and automotive manufacturing.

He shares a love of horses with me. As a young boy, we would ride and I would turn in my saddle, looking back, and say, "Will, are you OK, honey?" Now when we ride, he turns in his saddle, looking back, and says, "Dad, are you OK?"

On the last day of our annual Tejas Vaquero trail ride in the hill country of Texas is a rodeo. A few years back, Will won "All Around Cowboy," with a buckle and saddle to prove it. Yes, Dad was proud.

When Will was twelve, we were invited on a father-son hunt at a friend's ranch in South Texas. We joined another father-son duo flying in the dad's private plane, landing on the ranch's runway.

It was a great three-day weekend. We hunted in the morning and afternoon in a deer blind, and Will got his first deer. During the day, the boys, entertained by the owner, would take pistols to the garbage dump and shoot armadillos and cans, and practice archery. At night, we sat around the campfire with all the other fathers and sons, telling tall tales.

Returning to Houston, I asked Will, "With all the fun things you did—getting your first deer, pistol shooting, riding in a private plane—what was the most fun you had?"

Will's response: "Sitting in the deer blind with you, Dad." Yes, a big lump in my throat.

His greatest qualities? He is a wonderful son and brother.

25

Emily

WHEN THE PHONE RINGS AND WAKES YOU from a deep sleep, you first wonder: "What time is it?" When you see it is 1:30 in the morning, you first hope it is a wrong number; then you think, *This may not be good.* I reached across Anne and answered the phone. It was early Sunday, August 27, 1996.

The voice on the phone said, "This is Hermann Hospital Life Flight. Is this the Conner family that lives in River Oaks?"

"Yes," I responded.

Life Flight: "Your daughter Emily is in the emergency room."

"What happened to her?" My throat was catching.

Life Flight: "I'm not able to give you the details, but you should come to the hospital."

I turned to Anne: "I don't know what's happened, but we still have her."

We raced to the emergency room to see our nineteen-year-old daughter. It is all a blur now, but we learned that Emily had been in a diving accident and sustained a spinal cord injury. The doctor showed us an X-ray. I later learned that she had crushed her C5 and C6 vertebrae. Yes, she would be paralyzed. However, the doctors could not say to what extent.

In my mind, this could not be happening. She was supposed to leave for the University of Denver on a dance scholarship in five days.

We entered the ICU, where Emily opened her eyes from a drug-induced sleep. Let Emily tell you what happened:

> As I awoke, I heard many disturbing yet familiar sounds, but not one sound put me at ease. Then I heard the soft whisper of my father's voice. I was unable to make out where I was. Startled, I heard a man announcing that I was awake. Slowly, I was coming into consciousness. I could vaguely see several people around me, and I began to realize that the disturbing sounds I was hearing were machines.
>
> There was commotion and various hands on my body, but I felt no touch. A few minutes seemed to pass. I was later informed those minutes were days during which I was immobile. My nose began to itch, but my arm did not move and, therefore, my hand was unable to scratch it. At this point I was completely unaware of what lay ahead.
>
> I was unable to move my body, but my eyes frantically searched for the face that went with my father's whisper that I had heard just a moment before. I tried to call out, but I was mute. All I could hear were those damn machines. Never have I been so terrified. After a while, I figured out that my wrist could move just enough to hit the railing on the side of the bed. I thought

no one would ever be able to hear me, and I began to cry.

The rest of my stay in the ICU remained quite vague until I awoke to my mother's warm, familiar face and comforting smile. Her hand stroked my forehead. That was the moment I looked down to see my father grasping my waist, and his tears falling on my gown.

Was I still dreaming? My father appeared to be holding me tightly, but I could only see him. I closed my eyes as tightly as I possibly could and tried to feel his arms, his grasp, his tears—anything would do. I could not feel anything and, again, I began to cry.

Shortly thereafter, I was introduced to Dr. Ansel. He was very cordial, but the expression on his face was very serious. My father popped out of his chair and grabbed my hand. Although I could not feel it, I was comforted. Dr. Ansel told me I had been in an accident. Right then, I began to recall the instances that brought me to this point.

It had been a hot August day as dusk hit the water in Galveston Bay. We pulled up into a private little place where our party would not disturb the other boaters enjoying the nice quiet evening. There was music and laughter, but I was not concerned with the activities of others.

My boyfriend Matt and I were embracing, talking about my move to Colorado. Though I was thrilled by the thought, my heart was not quite ready. So, with a few tears welling up, I decided to go for a swim. My actions were sudden.

Matt looked up as I was throwing him my dress and diving into the water. I heard his panicked voice yelling, *"NO!"* realizing I was jumping into shallow water.

It is seared in my memory: Emily being wheeled to surgery to stabilize her neck. The nurses had spread her beautiful blonde hair across the back of her pillow. Our many friends in the ICU waiting area gasped. She was so lovely.

Two weeks later, doctors transferred Emily to The Institute for Rehabilitation and Research (TIRR), a world-famous hospital known for its expertise in the rehabilitation of patients with paralysis, traumatic brain injury, and stroke. Founded by Dr. William Spencer in the early 1950s to treat polio patients, the hospital evolved to the preeminent position it has today.

Emily started her physical therapy and occupational therapy. Over the twelve weeks in TIRR, she began to experience some recovery. Her biceps started to work. Then one day, one of the therapists happily announced, "Her triceps are kicking in." This meant her arms had complete movement. Soon, her trunk regained strength.

Positive things were happening. Then came the meeting with the doctor.

He explained to Emily, putting one hand at waist level, "Emily, this is where you are." He raised his hand to his throat. "Emily, this is normal." Then he lowered his hand to a middle position, between the high and low. "Emily, in about six months, you will regain some improvement, then you will be here the rest of your life."

He had just robbed Emily of the best medicine there is: hope.

As the nurse wheeled her out of the room with Anne and me behind her, she turned to us, tears in her eyes, and said, "They won't ever say that to patients like me again."

Emily was at TIRR for three months. The outpouring of love from our many friends was overwhelming. Her room was filled with posters and balloons. People constantly visited her. She had just graduated from Episcopal High School. Her friends who were off to college took turns coming to see her every weekend for the following year. Other parents' feelings for our situation were palpable.

Claude Payne, the bishop for the Episcopal Diocese of Texas, called me one day to ask that I provide legal assistance to someone very close to him. Although the legal problem he gave me was somewhat complicated, it was successfully resolved. Bishop Payne called to thank me and wanted to pay my bill. I told him it was my pleasure to help but it would be nice if he paid my bill in a different manner. I told him about Emily. Would he come to TIRR and perform a healing service? He graciously accepted my request.

It was an impressive sight when the bishop of Texas walked into the hospital in his full regalia, black robe, purple and white sashes, and a large gold cross hanging from his neck. He was very sweet with Emily and conducted the service from the prayer book.

Emily improved.

This beautiful girl was at TIRR until November 1996. When she came home, Anne was her primary caretaker during the day. We hired nursing students to cover the night. The mother–daughter relationship had been experiencing the anxiety of Emily leaving for Denver. Because of Emily's care requirements, it was almost like having an infant again. With her mother's insistence and Emily's determination, things would improve dramatically. It just took time.

One fortunate irony was that when Anne was in her early twenties, she had been engaged to a young man who had been in a boating accident. He sustained the exact injury as Emily. Anne stayed with her fiancé for quite some time and moved to

Amarillo, where he lived. Though the engagement ended, because of this experience, Anne knew exactly what was happening with Emily and the possibilities that lay ahead. There is no doubt that Emily's accomplishments were significant because of Anne's guidance, insistence, and decisions.

Anne's first announcement was that Emily would apply to the University of St. Thomas for the spring semester. Emily explained to her mother that people like her did nothing in their first year of paralysis. Anne told Emily that she would get on with her young life.

St. Thomas was exceptionally accommodating to Emily. They moved the class locations if the scheduled buildings were not wheelchair accessible.

Anne pushed Emily to stay involved with school and friends, and she did.

The Houston Livestock Show and Rodeo is the largest in the world. Anne and I were on committees, and I was a director of the show. Our children grew up going to the rodeo. We had many friends there who loved us. Anne knew the rodeo would be good for Emily, though Emily was unsure. Her self-esteem had taken a beating.

We persevered and took Emily there many nights once the 1997 show came around. To Emily's amazement, practically everyone appeared to be hovering over her, showering her with love and affection.

One night, something special happened. Jerry Andrew was a friend who was paralyzed as a young woman, and she raised three daughters from a wheelchair. She was proud and independent and had become the first female vice president of the rodeo. All show officers customarily ride in the grand entry—the first part of any rodeo—circling the arena and waving at the spectators. A special wagon was designed for Jerry to allow her to do the same in her wheelchair. One night, she insisted that Emily take her place, knowing it would be a boost to her mental healing.

Anne and I went down to the arena floor. We will always recall standing behind the bucking chutes and watching our young, paralyzed daughter in the wagon, waving at the crowd. With tears streaming down our faces, we knew her confidence was returning.

While I thought Emily would live with us forever, Anne had a different idea. She wanted Emily to be independent. In 1998, we bought her a house. We hired attendants to help Emily and drive her wheelchair-equipped van. It was just a matter of time before Emily got a van she could drive, making her more independent. She was also fortunate to have roommates. They would go out at night, just like other young women.

She graduated from the University of St. Thomas in 2002, then enrolled in South Texas College of Law, completing her law degree in 2006. She found employment in the executive department of Goodwill Industries. Today, Emily is the senior manager of compliance with responsibility over forty-three stores and 1,800 employees.

In 2015, she married Peter Hempel, who adores her. Emily is independent, confident, and successful.

26

The TIRR Emily Endowment

THERE IS ANOTHER CHAPTER TO EMILY'S JOURNEY that made her quite a celebrity in Houston. Toward the end of Emily's stay at TIRR Hospital, the chairman of the board, Howard Wolfe, came to her room and said, "Emily, I have a dream that in your lifetime we will find a cure for spinal cord injury." He then explained that he had been in talks with the three medical schools in the Houston area: Baylor College of Medicine, UT Houston, and UTMB Galveston. He was hoping for something unheard of: that the three medical schools would do collaborative research. Scientists can be very protective of their work. But this collaboration would unite them to find a cure for spinal cord injury.

Howard said that he was getting letters from all three schools agreeing to the collaboration and research, then added, "Emily, we need one million dollars in seed money. That way we can prove to the large-money foundations that we are serious."

Emily, lying in her hospital bed, did not miss a beat. "My family will do that." Anne and I looked in surprise at each other.

But we knew it could happen. The TIRR Emily Endowment came to life.

Fourteen months after Emily's accident, Hand in Hand with Hope held its first gala to benefit the TIRR Emily Endowment. Nine hundred and fifty tickets sold out the event before the first invitation was mailed. Jerry Jeff Walker was the entertainment. Live auction prizes included an African safari, a horse, a cruise, hunts on South Texas ranches, and two trips to Opryland. The event netted $600,000. It was a fantastic success.

Milby and John Dunn were two of Emily's best friends in their teenage years. Their father was Dow Dunn, head of the Dunn Foundation. A few weeks after the gala, Dow called Emily. "Emily, I heard you need to raise a million dollars, but you're short." Emily told Dow that was true. He responded, "Why don't I give you another $600,000 so you can get your show on the road?"

On August 26, 1997, with a million-plus dollars of seed money, Howard Wolfe held a news conference to announce the formation of Mission Connect, a collaboration of the three Houston medical schools to find a cure for spinal cord injuries. With Emily by his side, Howard said, "Spinal cord injury treatments will be to the Texas Medical Center in the first half of the twenty-first century what open heart surgery was in the second half of the twentieth century."

Emily, quite literally, became the rock star for Mission Connect.

Some publications that featured her, the TIRR Emily Endowment, and Mission Connect: two front-page articles in the *Houston Chronicle*, *Texas Medical Center News*, the *River Oaks Magazine*, the *St. Thomas University Magazine*, *Inside Houston Magazine*, and the *River Oaks Examiner*.

Today, Mission Connect has twenty institutions internationally working on cures for spinal cord and traumatic brain injuries, with 120 scientists collaborating on cutting-edge research.

And the doctor who took her hope away at TIRR in 1996? Emily saw him a few years later and asked if he still told his patients that there was no hope. He replied, "No, I tell them there is a lot of work being done to find a cure, and there are no guarantees, but one day …"

Through Scott McCarter—a young, paralyzed man—Emily learned of a camp for young "plegics" in Newport, Rhode Island: Shake-a-Leg. Emily enrolled in the program in the summer of 1999. It was the vision of a wealthy Providence native, Paul Callahan. Paul was paralyzed as a young man and recognized the need to improve the quality of life for young disabled people.

Shake-a-Leg activities included exercises, games, sailing, and social interactions. The dormitory was in one of the old restored "cottages" (compared to the mansions in New York that served as their owners' primary residences) in Newport. The gym was some two blocks away, uphill.

Going to Shake was a big and frightening adventure for Emily, her first time leaving home since her injury. She was nervous and hesitant to go. She went at Anne's insistence on the condition that she would only stay the first week of a five-week program. The second day Emily was there, she said she was staying the entire duration.

During her first summer, she improved dramatically. Brother Will was amazed to see how she was doing when he arrived from Houston. At one point, she was pushing her wheelchair up a rather steep hill. Will, walking beside her, jumped in to help. Kristy Hart, the program director, said, "Leave her alone, Will."

His retort: "Not on a hill this steep."

Kristy added, "Let her go!"

Of course, she made it to the top.

Emily was at Shake-a-Leg for two summers, and those experiences moved her forward, in her own words, "in body, mind, and spirit." She returned for two more summers to mentor new participants as they moved forward with their lives. Robbie Pierce, who has MS and has been a consultant at Shake-a-Leg for many years, said, "I just love Emily; her energy and smile could electrify a small city."

In 2003, Paul called Emily and said, "Congratulations, you are the Lauren Meany Spirit Award recipient." The award is given after summer camp to an individual who has made a significant contribution to Shake-a-Leg and to their community, which in Emily's case came through Mission Connect.

A crew came to Houston to video Emily at home, conducting interviews with friends, Will, Anne, Dr. Guy Clifton—the medical director of Mission Connect—and me to be played at the Newport banquet honoring Emily.

President George H. W. Bush gave a videotaped introduction about Emily. After the meal, the video was played. In the banquet room filled with hundreds of people, you could hear a pin drop when his face appeared on the giant screen. "Barbara and I wish we could be in Newport with you tonight as you honor Emily Conner …"

The Lauren Meany Spirit Award event wasn't Emily's only connection with President Bush. July 26, 2000, marked the tenth anniversary of the passage of the Americans with Disabilities Act. A celebration was held in Houston. President Bush gave remarks, and one of the speakers said, "What Lincoln did for the slaves, President Bush did for people with disabilities."

As part of the celebration, the Spirit of the ADA torch was passed in a hand-to-hand relay of disabled athletes through twenty-three cities, ending in Washington, DC. On stage with the president, Emily held the torch that he lit. In turn, she handed it to the first paraplegic wheelchair racer.

President Bush sent Anne a note following the ceremony: "I am glad to be a tiny part of courageous Emily's life."

We all are.

EPILOGUE

It's Been Quite a Ride

WHEN I STARTED THIS PROJECT, IT WAS a lark. The more I wrote, the more serious the project became. I was fortunate to have a muse who gave me positive encouragement, insisting that I keep writing, and she has my sincere thanks.

This project has brought back many wonderful memories. How fortunate I have been for my life experiences, a wonderful family, knowing great lawyers and judges, having clients who were loyal and followed my advice——most of the time. And there were the miscreants I met along the way, and the adventures in and out of the courtroom.

Thanks for coming along with me.

Tom Conner
Santa Fe, New Mexico
2025

Acknowledgments

AFFECTIONATE THANKS GO TO ANGIE BYRNES, the best paralegal in Texas; Ruth Rodriguez, my wonderful assistant; and Tina Maier, my office manager who kept my mind at peace. These ladies made my life and practice easier and made me look smart in the process. In our years together, we never had a harsh word. They may have had to correct me, but they were always perfect.

Gratitude and thanks to my law partners, James Patrick Smith and Steve Lindamood. Both great lawyers and wonderful friends.

Appreciation is extended to Red to Black Editing for their helpful suggestions.

The following authors deserve credit for the background provided for my research. I recommend their books to the reader: Carlton Smith for his well-researched book about the Angleton case, *Death in Texas*; Gary Cartwright for his excellent book about Priscilla and Cullen Davis, *Blood Will Tell*; and Jerry Argovitz's autobiography, *Super Agent*.

www.ingramcontent.com/pod-product-compliance
Lightning Source LLC
Chambersburg PA
CBHW070240090526
44586CB00035B/1075